GEORGE PÉREZ

FREDERICK LUIS ALDAMA, SERIES EDITOR

GEORGE
PÉREZ

PATRICK L. HAMILTON

UNIVERSITY PRESS OF MISSISSIPPI / JACKSON

The University Press of Mississippi is the scholarly publishing agency of the Mississippi Institutions of Higher Learning: Alcorn State University, Delta State University, Jackson State University, Mississippi State University, Mississippi University for Women, Mississippi Valley State University, University of Mississippi, and University of Southern Mississippi.

www.upress.state.ms.us

Title page portrait by Antony Hare

The University Press of Mississippi is a member of the Association of University Presses.

Library of Congress Cataloging-in-Publication Data

Names: Hamilton, Patrick Lawrence, author.
Title: George Pérez / Patrick L. Hamilton.
Other titles: Biographix.
Description: Jackson : University Press of Mississippi, 2024. | Series: Biographix | Includes bibliographical references and index.
Identifiers: LCCN 2024003510 (print) | LCCN 2024003511 (ebook) | ISBN 9781496851253 (hardback) | ISBN 9781496851246 (trade paperback) | ISBN 9781496851239 (epub) | ISBN 9781496851222 (epub) | ISBN 9781496851215 (pdf) | ISBN 9781496851208 (pdf)
Subjects: LCSH: Pérez, George, 1954–2022. | Pérez, George, 1954–2022—Criticism and interpretation. | Hispanic American cartoonists. | Cartoonists—United States. | Hispanic American artists. | Superheroes in comics. | Comic books, strips, etc.—United States—History and criticism.
Classification: LCC PN6727.P463 Z68 2024 (print) | LCC PN6727.P463 (ebook) | DDC 741.5/973—dc23/eng/20240223
LC record available at https://lccn.loc.gov/2024003510
LC ebook record available at https://lccn.loc.gov/2024003511

British Library Cataloging-in-Publication Data available

To Frederick

CONTENTS

ACKNOWLEDGMENTS

The first comic book I remember buying was *Avengers* (1963) no. 164, which sported a George Pérez cover and was the start of my forty-plus years of fandom. Having the opportunity to write a book on Pérez and in particular revisit his work in *Avengers* and *The New Teen Titans*—titles I've followed for decades—was an immense joy and privilege. I hope this book does justice to Pérez and what he did in and for comics, as well as spur further investigations into his work.

I owe an immense debt to Frederick Luis Aldama, to whom this book is dedicated, for his ceaseless efforts on my behalf for over twenty years at this point. The opportunities he has provided me—including the invitation to write this book—have truly shaped my career, and I cannot ever thank him enough for all he has done.

I similarly need to thank Allan W. Austin, professor of history and government at Misericordia University. Allan read early drafts of many of the chapters and provided feedback that was instrumental in helping me pull them together into their final form, but more importantly, he is my constant friend (which, admittedly, isn't always easy).

I would also like to thank everyone at the University Press of Mississippi for their efforts in helping bring this book to its realization. This list includes Frederick, obviously, as series editor for the Biographix series; Lisa McMurtray, associate editor for Biographix; Michael C. Martella, who answered numerous questions as I was putting together the final manuscript; Amy Atwood and Joey Brown in marketing; Todd Lape and Pete Halverson in production and design; Valerie Jones in editing; and many others at UPM that I am deeply grateful to for their role in shepherding this project. A special thanks goes to Laura J. Vollmer for all her work copyediting the manuscript and responding to my questions.

I likewise am thankful to the individuals who reviewed and provided important feedback on the original manuscript of this book, all of which aided in making it better. Similarly, I presented very early work on what would eventually evolve into chapter 1 at the 2018 Mid-Atlantic Popular Culture Conference in Baltimore, Maryland, and appreciate the feedback I received at that stage.

This project received a great deal of support from my institution, Misericordia University, in the form of research grants during the summers of 2018 and 2019, research release during the 2020–21 academic year, and my sabbatical in spring 2022, during which the first draft of the manuscript was completed. My thanks to both the Faculty Research Grants Committee and the Faculty Status Committee for their support of this project and my research in general.

Finally, I'd like to thank my family: my parents, Bob and Dianna, who stoked my love of comics with trips to comic book stores and conventions; my sisters, Julie and Valerie, who I love dearly; all of my nieces and nephews—Abby, Sam, Shelby, and Paddy; and, of course, my beagle, Leia, who I got while working on this project and is a very good girl.

GEORGE PÉREZ

The Invisible Artist

I used to feel a little bit peeved whenever I would see a
review on a book I had drawn and somebody was com-
menting all about the story, no one was really mentioning
the art to any degree. . . . Then I realized that's exactly what
I'm supposed to do. It's like a director not calling too much
attention to himself by being so glitzy that people *notice*
he's directing. Storytelling should be dynamic, forceful. If
it's well drawn, great, but it should always be at the service
of a story.

—George Pérez quoted in Lawrence, *George Pérez*, 24

B orn in 1954 in the South Bronx to a mother and father who
migrated separately from Puerto Rico, George Pérez was one
of the most, if not the most, prominent Latinx comics creators—
rivaled only by fellow artist José Luis García-López—working
in the so-called "Bronze Age" of the 1970s and 1980s. Beginning
at Marvel with runs on lesser titles like the Man-Wolf feature
in *Creatures on the Loose* (1971) and the Sons of the Tiger in the
black-and-white *The Deadly Hands of Kung Fu* (1974) magazine,
Pérez soon graduated to working on Marvel mainstays like *Fantastic Four* (1961) and *Avengers* (1963), the latter being where Pérez
most fully established his initial reputation as an artist. Making
the jump to DC in the early 1980s, Pérez was involved in two of
its most significant and successful relaunches. With writer Marv
Wolfman, Pérez took the failed Teen Titans franchise and made
The New Teen Titans (1980) into DC's best-selling title. Following

the universe-altering *Crisis on Infinite Earths* (1985) miniseries (likewise penned by him and Wolfman), Pérez undertook his most significant individual achievement in comics: the relaunch of *Wonder Woman* (1987), for which Pérez had a five-year run as writer and was, for the first two years, the primary artist. From there, regular comics work proved difficult for Pérez to maintain. But he still managed to produce important work as an "event comic" artist, perhaps best represented by series at Marvel such as *The Infinity Gauntlet* (1991) with Jim Starlin and *Hulk: Future Imperfect* (1992) with writer Peter David. His return to the regular artistic duties on *Avengers* (1998) with writer Kurt Busiek reinvigorated Pérez's career and introduced him and his art to a new generation of comic readers. In addition to this successful run, Pérez also drew the long-delayed and seemingly never-to-happen *JLA/Avengers* (2003) crossover that finally brought DC's and Marvel's top hero teams together in one dazzling storyline. The 2000s saw Pérez continue to pop up here and there at both Marvel and DC, as well as branch out into new endeavors, such as various fantasy titles at CrossGen and his own creator-owned series *George Pérez's Sirens* (2016)—his final work before retiring at the start of 2019 out of health considerations—at Boom! Studios. Passing away from pancreatic cancer in May 2022, George Pérez was a formative force in generating the look and feel of late twentieth-century superhero comics.

However, Pérez's significance within comics often falls short of full recognition. For example, in 2017, he was one of sixteen nominees short-listed for the Hall of Fame of the Will Eisner Comic Industry Awards. Summing up Pérez's accomplishments, the nomination described how he "developed a reputation as the artist who liked to draw group books" ("Hall of Fame"). The nomination also checked off various titles he had worked on in his career: at Marvel, *Fantastic Four*, *Inhumans* (1975), and *Avengers*; for DC, *The New Teen Titans*, *Wonder Woman*, and *Crisis on Infinite Earths*. There is little here to compare to the accolades given to other nominees. Though Pérez was voted by fans into the Hall of Fame, the nomination's distillation of his career feels paltry at best. This is, sadly, all too common. For all that he has done, George Pérez has generally not been seen as a unique contributor to comics style and storytelling.

What recognition Pérez has received can be found outside the comics industry proper: some of the most recent films in both the DC Extended Universe (DCEU) and the Marvel Cinematic Universe (MCU) owe a deep debt to Pérez. The final credits of *Wonder Woman* (2017) list Pérez above and thus separately from the rest of the comic creators under "Special Thanks to," the only one in this list to be so singled out and second only to Wonder Woman's creators—William Moulton Marston as well as "The Marston Family"[1]—in the entirety of these credits. This distinction speaks to how the film bases itself in the early issues of Pérez's *Wonder Woman*. The film's design of both the Amazon home of Themyscira and the depiction of the Amazons themselves, both in their general appearance and lack of overt sexualization, is very much in keeping with what Pérez accomplished; as well, several of the Amazon characters Pérez individualized in his run—such as Antiope, Menalippe, and Phillipus—are named characters in the film. Plot elements from Pérez's first six-issue arc on the series also exist in the film. The comic and film send Diana to "Man's World" to confront Ares, the Greek god of war, who is manipulating humankind toward war (in the case of the comics, this happens in the context of the Cold War in the late 1980s, while the film transplants the conflict to World War I). In both, Wonder Woman battles and defeats Ares while Steve Trevor (aged up in the comic so as not to present a potential love interest for Diana) works to successfully defuse another attack; he survives in the comic, while perishing in the film. In both, Wonder Woman allies herself not only with Trevor but also with a ragtag group of allies: Etta Candy is present in both the film and comic, but whereas Wonder Woman's WWI cohorts include (in addition to Trevor) the Blackfoot called "Chief," the Moroccan Sameer/"Sammy," and the Scottish sniper Charlie, in the comic, she teams up alongside Trevor and

Candy with Harvard professor Julia Kapatelis and Trevor's friend and colleague Col. Matthew Michaelis.

The MCU owes a more implicit but no less significant debt to Pérez. The film most directly based in his work is 2018's *Avengers: Infinity War*, a loose adaptation of the limited series *The Infinity Gauntlet* written by Jim Starlin and illustrated by Pérez through the opening pages of issue 4. In the first issue of that series, the Silver Surfer crashes through the window of Dr. Strange's Sanctum Sanctorum to warn of the danger Thanos presents, a moment the film directly homages, swapping the Surfer for Bruce Banner/the Hulk. Likewise, Nebula's capture and torture by Thanos is another beat that the film directly translates from what Pérez drew. But perhaps more evocative of Pérez is what a film like *Avengers: Infinity War* accomplished in bringing together the various properties the MCU comprises: teams like the Avengers and the Guardians of the Galaxy, as well as individual heroes like Ant-Man, Dr. Strange, Black Panther, Captain Marvel, and Sony's Spider-Man. A common talking point about *Avengers: Infinity War*, both before and after its release, was the sheer number of characters included in not only the film but also, at times, in individual scenes. This, too, is a common refrain about Pérez. Part of the attraction of his art is, for readers, to see and, for Pérez, to illustrate a panoply of brightly costumed heroes from DC or Marvel (or, in the case of *JLA/Avengers*, both). Films like *Avengers: Infinity War* and subsequent MCU entries like *Avengers: Endgame* (2019), *Spider-Man: No Way Home* (2021), and *Doctor Strange in the Multiverse of Madness* (2022) evoke the same kind of thrill as a Pérez-drawn comic. Sprawling in plot and dynamic in visuals, these films evoke what are signatures of Pérez's work.

If film recognizes Pérez, another realm outside the comics industry—comics scholarship—has largely not. As Marc Singer aptly sums up, "As a prolific creator whose bestselling titles and diverse characters have been adapted across multiple media, he [Pérez] has exerted a powerful influence on the superhero genre. . . . Yet despite his many contributions to the comics industry,

Pérez has generally been ignored by comics scholars" ("George Pérez" 289). Multiple examples of this neglect exist. In *Wonder Women: Feminisms and Superheroes* (2004), Lillian S. Robinson identifies what she terms a postmodern phase in the depiction of Wonder Woman as coinciding with the character's post-*Crisis* reboot. However, she fails to mention Pérez as the one most responsible for this new direction. Furthermore, Robinson's analysis of this phase focuses not on Pérez's stint on *Wonder Woman* but a later run by John Byrne (86, 130–32). Similarly, Joan Ormrod discounts Pérez's contribution to this run. She not only lists Pérez last among the contributors to this revision but also describes him as only penciling the series until issue 19, when she claims he took over the writing (Ormrod 119). In actuality, Pérez was a co-plotter of the series from the start, working with Greg Potter, who coplotted and scripted the first two issues of the series, and then Len Wein, who scripted the series from issues 3 to 16; with issue 17, Pérez became the sole writer, as well as continuing as the primary artist of the series.

Pérez has similarly been discounted in other accounts of comics history. When talking about artists at Marvel who followed in the wake of—and thus both demonstrate and moderate the influence of—Jack Kirby, Charles Hatfield mentions whom many see as the mainstays of the 1970s Marvel "Bullpen"—Neal Adams, John Buscema, Walter Simonson, and John Byrne—but leaves out Pérez, who is a contemporary of this quartet and often seen as a rival to Byrne. Pérez has also been absented from discussions of specific runs on titles of which he was the artist. Singer, for instance, notes Pérez's complete absence from the MLA International Bibliography, even though Marv Wolfman is cited multiple times for work they cocreated ("George Pérez" 289). Similarly, two of the essays in the collection *The Ages of the Avengers* (2014) deal with eras of the team during which Pérez was the artist; however, they actually give credit to the writers for visual aspects of the team. Jason Sacks, discussing the late 1970s Korvac Saga for which Pérez was initially the artist, credits not him but writer Jim Shooter with the following: "it is always clear who the characters are on each page. Characters are almost always introduced in an unambiguous manner, and an attempt is always made to differentiate the heroes both by their look and their personality" (34). Todd Steven Burroughs's discussion of how Christopher Priest's version of Black Panther was incorporated into the Avengers team in the late 1990s lauds writer Kurt Busiek for this, noting specifically how "Panther is in the background, in silhouette, his new energy daggers drawn" (114). In both these cases, credit for visual aspects of the page, like appearance and positioning, is given to the writers Pérez collaborated with rather than the artist himself.

The factors contributing to this neglect of Pérez are many. Singer provides a thorough litany of these complications, beginning with various tendencies in comics scholarship to privilege realistic or neorealistic works over superhero comics, as well as to oversimplify comic book production in ways that privilege writers over artists ("George Pérez" 289–90). Other factors stem from aspects of the comic industry itself. Pérez reached his initial artistic peak just as works like Alan Moore and Dave Gibbons's *Watchmen* (1986) and Frank Miller's *The Dark Knight Returns* (1986) appeared. These works, in their respective deconstructions of traditional superhero tropes, consequently positioned traditional superhero art, and thus artists like Pérez, as old-fashioned or outmoded. The limited availability of Pérez's work in print or digital collections has been another factor compromising his legacy, though this has, as of late, been significantly remedied (290).

Several of these factors as well as others that impact Pérez's standing as a creator merit further unpacking. For Pérez, the preeminence given to writers over artists has been particularly problematic. The vast majority of comics work Pérez produced was collaborative in nature, with Pérez often relegated to "artist" or "penciler" in the credits as well as in the minds of most readers. However, the reality is more complicated. There are works in which Pérez's contributions were largely artistic: his run on *Avengers* with Kurt Busiek, for instance, about which he explicitly stated he did not want any role in writing/plotting the series, and *The Infinity Gauntlet*, which was the culmination of a long-running storyline in writer Jim Starlin's *Silver Surfer* (1987) title. However, there are others for which he assumed more of a cocreator role with the writer. The clearest example of such is his work with Marv Wolfman on both *The New Teen Titans* and *Crisis on Infinite Earths*. Though the special preview of the first title in *DC Comics Presents* no. 26 credits Wolfman as writer and Pérez and inker Dick Giordano as "illustrators," from the first issue of the actual series, Wolfman and Pérez are identified as "co-creators," which continues throughout the first fifty issues of the series and then changes to "co-creators and co-editors" of the title's second volume, which ended Pérez's first run on the property. Similarly, though Pérez began *Crisis* solely as its artist, he eventually shared with Wolfman coplotting/cocreator duties on this title as well. Unfortunately, the greater role Pérez played in creating these works is not always recognized. One has only to look at the credits for the collected versions of these works to see that this oversimplification persists. The first three volumes of the Omnibus collection of *The New Teen Titans*—which together comprise Pérez's complete initial run on the title—list Wolfman as "writer" and Pérez (along with the various inkers and guest pencilers) only as "artist," as does the Deluxe Edition of *Crisis*.

Likewise, a predilection toward auteur theory in comics scholarship, which Singer explicates, has worked against Pérez. Imported from film, auteur theory, when applied to comics, has put emphasis on creators that both write and draw comics. A few examples of such "comic auteurs" include Art Spiegelman, Marjane Satrapi, Alison Bechdel, Joe Sacco, and Los Bros Hernandez, all of whom work in realistic or neorealistic modes, which comics scholars have tended to gravitate toward (Singer, "George Pérez" 305). Perhaps fewer names spring to mind of such auteurs within superhero comics, but certainly creators like Jack Kirby with *Eternals* (1976) at Marvel and the Fourth World (1970) books at DC, Frank Miller with Marvel's *Daredevil* (1964) and DC's *The Dark Knight Returns*,

John Byrne on *Superman* (1987) for DC and *Fantastic Four* at Marvel, and Walter Simonson's run on *Thor* (1966) for Marvel are examples. These last two—Byrne and Simonson—make a useful comparison with Pérez. All three not only were among the leading artists at Marvel and/or DC in the 1980s but also had their influential runs around the same time: Byrne on *Fantastic Four* between 1981 and 1986, Simonson on *Thor* from 1983 until 1987, and Pérez on *Wonder Woman* from 1987 to 1992.

However, despite each helming their respective titles for roughly four to five years, the extent to which they served as both writer and primary pencil artist varies, particularly in the case—and to the detriment—of Pérez. Byrne, for example, was writer and artist for all but one issue during his stint on *Fantastic Four*, while Simonson served in both capacities for roughly two-thirds of his *Thor* run. This is not the case with Pérez. To begin with, Pérez came on to the title's development with another creator—Greg Potter—not only lined up as writer for the series but also to whom Pérez credits such aspects of the series as the Amazons being reincarnations of women murdered by men throughout time, Ares as the first threat and what prompts Diana's departure for "Man's World," and, once there, establishing Diana in Boston, Massachusetts, Potter's hometown (Baker 58–59). Potter left the series after its second issue, but Pérez split writing duties with industry veteran Len Wein through issue 16, with Pérez plotting and Wein scripting each issue. As of no. 17, Pérez was finally given full rein on *Wonder Woman*—plotting, scripting, and penciling the series—but this only lasted through issue 24, after which Pérez no longer drew the series. Thus, unlike Byrne and Simonson, who have several years of issues they both wrote and drew, the number of issues of *Wonder Woman* about which the same can be said about Pérez is only eight. As a result, it is much easier to see Byrne and Simonson as comic auteurs—given the size of their contribution to their respective titles (and, in Byrne's case, others, including *Superman*)—than Pérez.

Factors pertaining to the production of comics in general and superhero comics in particular also contribute to an underestimation of Pérez's work. For one, Pérez came to prominence within a very different era of comics production, particularly at Marvel. By the 1970s, when Pérez began his work in comics, writers held profound sway over their narratives, veering away from the "Marvel style" plotting of the 1960s that saw artists like Kirby and Steve Ditko drawing entire issues from, at times, the most minimal of plots. Pérez's earliest work had him paired with writers that in many ways served as mainstays at Marvel in the 1970s and 1980s: Bill Mantlo on *The Deadly Hands of Kung Fu* and Steve Englehart and Jim Shooter on *Avengers*. The latter two in particular seemed to wield a relatively strong hand when it came to storylines given their being responsible for several of the most significant "sagas" within *Avengers* history: Englehart penning both the Celestial Madonna Saga (*Avengers* nos. 129–35 plus *Giant-Size Avengers* nos. 2–4) and the Serpent Crown storyline (*Avengers* nos. 141–49), while Shooter helmed the famed Korvac Saga (*Avengers* nos. 167–77). Pérez's first stint on *Avengers* coincided with the start of Englehart's second epic and ended with Shooter's, and Pérez's influence on these narratives was limited. Englehart, Pérez says, had ideas and made decisions of his own; when it came to staging the fight scenes in the title, at least, Pérez usually "won out" (Baker 14). With Shooter, the writer's relatively new arrival at Marvel did give Pérez some greater latitude as Pérez credits him and writer David Michelinie, who also worked on *Avengers* during Pérez's time on the series, with allowing him to "become the *Avengers* artist," though the description of him being "allowed" still speaks to limits (26–27).

Adding to this are the artistic strictures Pérez labored under at Marvel. As Pérez himself points out, editors attempted to stamp out idiosyncratic aspects of his artwork in favor of a more conventional "house style." His first issue of *Avengers*—no. 141—exhibits those idiosyncrasies. During various sequences of heightened action—the Beast and Captain America taking on a squad of Roxxon thugs on pages 2 and 3, Thor and Moondragon traveling through time in pursuit of Kang the Conqueror on pages 10–12 (figure 0.1), and the Avengers' confrontation with the Squadron Supreme on pages 16–18—Pérez uses more diagonal page layouts and trapezoidal panels (Englehart et al. 307–8, 316–17, 320–22).[2] In the case of the scenes depicting Thor and Moondragon's pursuit of Kang, the altered layout reflects the differing reality they have entered. However, this tendency toward what Pérez himself characterizes as more "wild panel designs" and "wonky layouts" was curtailed by series editors who desired a much more conventionally gridded page (Baker 16). And the effect was fairly immediate as similar such layouts only somewhat pepper the pages of the next couple of issues before disappearing entirely until the start of the Korvac Saga, Shooter's cosmic plot as well as Pérez's stronger position as an artist likely allowing him to veer somewhat from the conventions of Marvel's "house style."

What all this adds up to is perhaps the quality of Pérez's art that has most significantly contributed to his unfortunate erasure from discussions of comics: its transparency. Charles Hatfield alludes to the general prevalence of this transparency within superhero comics when discussing what he terms a "misapprehension" of them: "that superheroes stories are best realized with a high degree of realism . . . and that therefore the litmus test of comic book art is its treatment of the realistically proportioned, classically formed, beautifully posed human figure" (63). Far from any kind of stylization, such an aesthetic calls for superhero comic book art to not call attention to itself and thus, in a sense, be seen through rather than seen. It is within such an aesthetic that Singer observes how an artist like Pérez finds himself in a double bind. As previously mentioned, Singer notes the privilege afforded to writing over art in comics as narrative, theme, and context have prevailed over artistic/aesthetic considerations in the pursuit of some notion of "literariness" ("George Pérez" 290). But this has an added impact on an artist like Pérez who exudes—or, perhaps more accurately,

Figure 0.1. Thor and Moondragon pursue Kang through time from *Avengers*, vol. 1, no. 143, 1976 (Englehart et al. 316).

is made to exude—what appears to be a more conventional style; he also became so skilled in that style that his own work is, to use a term from Singer, self-effacing (291). Adding to this is Pérez's own cognizance of this vexed position. On the one hand, as the quotation at the start of this introduction attests, he notes his frustration at how commenters neglect his artistic contributions; on the other hand, he states this as precisely the point of his art.

The invisibility this transparency produced is what this book's analysis of Pérez's work contributes to correcting. To accomplish this, it explicates some of what is significant and unique in his work, surveyed over the course of his life and career. As a result, the discussions that follow can be seen as efforts to reinsert Pérez and his work into various discourses within comics scholarship. The first of these efforts relates to Pérez's style of comic book art. Scholarly analysis of his art has been severely limited. Singer's discussion of Pérez within the context of Bronze Age comic book art is the most significant, locating him and his fellow artists within what Singer terms "classical narrative style," which subsumes formal aspects of the work to narrative in a way akin to Hollywood cinema ("George Pérez" 296). Besides Singer, there is also Robert C. Harvey, who credits Pérez with innovation only in "layout and composition" of the comic page and not in terms of narrative or time/action ("In Search of Perez's Storytelling" 58–62). Beyond these scholarly discussions, what largely contributes to an understanding of Pérez's art are his own comments provided in various interviews he has done over the length of his career. The discussion here seeks to expand upon these extant discussions and thus add to our understanding of how and what Pérez contributes to comic art and narrative. This effort begins by positioning Pérez, like other Bronze Age superhero artists, in relation to the work of Jack Kirby. While in some ways being more refined and thus contained than Kirby in his construction of the comic page, Pérez also presents a similar dynamism and sense of what Hatfield centers as "the sublime" in Kirby's work (qtd. in Singer, "George Pérez" 305). As well, Pérez's art can be seen as not only an instance of what Hatfield describes as "narrative drawing" but also as an embrace and maximization of the storyworld possibilities within comics (305).

Moving from these stylistic considerations, this reappraisal of Pérez continues by reinserting him into cultural discourses connected to comics. First among these discourses are those concerning race and disability, which Pérez contributed to through several characters he helped create. Regarding race, the characters include Marvel's Sons of the Tiger, White Tiger, and Triathlon along with DC's Cyborg. Cyborg also centers disability in his representation, as does a later Teen Titan, the mute Jericho. Though, in narrative terms, these characters more often than not replicate problematic conceptions or narratives concerning race and/or disability, Pérez can be seen as resisting and, at times, transcending those problematic narratives in his design and visualization of the comic page.

A similar trajectory exists within Pérez's work when it comes to gender. Though his *Wonder Woman* series is often singled out for its representation of gender, this work is ultimately continuous within a conscious effort to improve gender and in particular women's representation in comics, which increased as Pérez's career and abilities developed. This effort began during his first run on *The New Teen Titans*, in which Pérez altered his style to better differentiate male and female body types, and features next in *Wonder Woman*, in which, as writer and artist, he strived (not always with success) to eschew both narrative and visual tropes and traps related to women in particular. Conscious attention to gender persists even through the spottier parts of Pérez's career before becoming sustained once again in both his second *Avengers* stint and his final work, *George Pérez's Sirens*; in both, Pérez again grounded his work in his concerns about comics' representation of gender and women, which are ultimately a bedrock within his career. That career, too, is one that, despite Pérez's self-professed transparency, much more apparently and variedly contributes to comics.

CHAPTER ONE

Play and Possibility on the Comic Book Page

> To me, if you're doing tiers of equal size, then you're just doing comic strips that are stacked on top of each other. Comic strips are bound because they are horizontal and are pretty much restricted to that configuration. A comic book is built on a vertical configuration. You can play a lot more with it.
>
> —George Pérez quoted in
> Nolen-Weathington, *Modern Masters* 27

Within the above quotation, George Pérez expresses both the value of his work for the study of comic book art and narrative as well as why it has gone too much unrecognized. Pérez describes himself as maximizing what can be done within the axes of the comic book page, which has the horizontal dimension of the comic strip but also a vertical dimension that distinguishes it. In the way he aspires to take full advantage of the space of the comic book page, Pérez speaks to what is innovative about his art, as his stated desire to "play a lot more with it" gestures at pushing the page toward its potential. Implicitly, however, Pérez casts himself as an artist who works within the comic book page's configuration and thus its "rules." The vertical dimension adds to what the comic book page can do versus the horizontal strip, but that page is still, for Pérez, "bound" by these two dimensions. He positions himself as an artist who does as much within the "rules" of the page as he can rather than one who breaks them and thus revolutionizes the page.

However, this aspect of Pérez's art can be thought of as less a bug and more as a feature. Rather than being impinged upon by various constraints—self- or industry-imposed[3]—Pérez's work is defined by his conscious effort to stretch (in some cases, quite literally) the possibilities of the comic book page. How he does this is two-pronged. First, it occurs in his construction of the physical comic page in terms of its design, layout, composition, etc. Second, and perhaps more significantly, is what Pérez's art accomplishes in terms of narrative. One of Pérez's most signature contributions is in his construction and creation of "storyworlds." Not only does Pérez, over the course of his career, surround the characters and events in his comics with a palpable sense of the world they inhabit, but he also embraces the outré elements of fantasy and wonder that were only possible on the comic page up until very recently. In this, Pérez exhibits what Frederick Aldama describes as the "will to style," "the responsibility of the creator (or creators) in understanding well the building blocks of reality that they are reconstructing as well as the degree of presence of a willful use of skills and technical devices to give shape to the making of new pop-cultural phenomena" (*Latinx Superheroes* 4). Pérez is both a builder of comic book pages and of comic book worlds that are intentional in playing with and thus maximizing possibilities unique to comic book pages and narratives.

These signatures of Pérez's comic book art developed over the course of many years, and thus it is worth briefly tracing the trajectory his career followed. Pérez's early years in the comics industry commenced with his stints on lesser-tier titles at Marvel like *The Deadly Hands of Kung Fu*, *Creatures on the Loose* (featuring Man-Wolf), and *Inhumans* before he graduated to more marquee titles like *Fantastic Four* and *Avengers*. Starting on the latter title with issue 141 in 1975, Pérez sustained a relationship with *Avengers* for the next five years despite coming and going from the title. His initial run on the title was from issue 141 to 155, for which Pérez contributed pencil art for roughly eleven of those fifteen issues. He came back to *Avengers* starting with no. 160, continuing (not uninterrupted) until his departure after issue 171 early on in the Korvac Saga; he returned for a brief third run from, except for one issue, no. 194 through no. 202. By the end of his time on *Avengers*, Pérez had contributed interior art to twenty-six monthly issues and two giant-sized annuals out of the sixty-plus issues published between his first and last, but that was enough for him to cement a lasting association with *Avengers*.

Pérez reached even further heights when he left Marvel for DC in the early 1980s; there, he completed legendary runs on *The New Teen Titans*, the universe-redefining *Crisis on Infinite Earths* (both with Marv Wolfman) and then as writer and artist on *Wonder Woman*. Following the end of his time at DC, however, Pérez's career reached a bit of a low point. Editorial interference and a lack of support tarnished the *War of the Gods* (1991) event series that was to cap his time on *Wonder Woman*. He likewise developed a reputation for not completing runs; a case in point was Marvel's *The Infinity Gauntlet* for which Pérez only held the art chores on the first three issues before passing the baton to artist Ron Lim partway through issue 4. Time eventually saw Pérez work to redeem his reputation, first by taking on full art duties for the two-issue prestige-format series *Hulk: Future Imperfect* with writer Peter David, serving as inker on a rebooted *Teen Titans* (1996) with writer Dan Jurgens, and then briefly writing Marvel's *Silver Surfer*. Fully redeeming Pérez, though, was his return and subsequent three-year run on *Avengers* with writer Kurt Busiek beginning in 1998, topped off, in many ways, by the release of *JLA/Avengers* (again with Busiek as writer) in 2003, a project long delayed and long associated with Pérez. The 2000s saw Pérez continue to work in comics, dipping his artistic toes into fantasy comics with Cross-Gen, completing a ten-issue stint on *The Brave and the Bold* (2007) with writer Mark Waid, and contributing to DC's relaunch of its universe with the New 52 as writer and layout artist on *Superman* (2011) and by sharing pencils with Kevin Maguire on a *Worlds' Finest* (2013) series featuring Power Girl and Huntress. He then penned his creator-owned series *George Pérez's Sirens* for Boom! Studios, which was completed in 2016.

The trajectory of Pérez's career also adds to the reasons for his neglect and underestimation. The early phases of Pérez's comics career put him at a couple of disadvantages. Though one can see Pérez developing into the artist he would become known as by the end of his first stint on *Avengers*, many of these issues and especially the work preceding it share a roughness resulting from how Pérez was learning to be a comic book artist as he went. His first issue of *The Deadly Hands of Kung Fu*, issue 6 from 1974, is a clear exhibit of this fact (and not just because of his being ill matched with inker Frank Springer). A salient example comes from page 6 of this issue's chapter of the Sons of the Tiger feature. The villainous Paan berates his men, just defeated by the Sons, in the second panel. One can just barely see a woman kneeling behind Paan's chair; three panels later, he now stands with his arm wrapped around her. The transition here—both in terms of Paan's standing and grabbing the woman, Emmy Jo—is jarring. The middle panel on the next page shows Pérez's weaknesses when it comes to perspective (figure 1.1). The scene shifts to Bob Diamond, the white member of the Sons, as Emmy Jo calls him, attempting to lure him into a trap. In the horizontal panel occupying the middle of the page, Diamond swings at a punching bag, the motion lines directing his fist forward and then up toward his right, but the bag is positioned behind his fist. The bag is also completely inert as Diamond hits it, showing no effect of his punch despite the coruscating lines indicating the intensity of the strike (Moench et al. 376, 377). An early effort at vertical panels is similarly mixed. In *Avengers* no. 143, Pérez uses a vertical panel on page 13 to depict Thor knocking Kang through the wall of his fortress; however, as Kang flies out and up from the fortress, he is drawn heading toward the bottom of the panel, creating a somewhat contradictory sense of movement (Englehart et al. 356). In these examples, Pérez can be seen as working through his limitations as a young artist.

Figure 1.1. Emmy Jo attempts to lure Bob Diamond into a trap from *Deadly Hands of Kung Fu*, no. 6, 1974 (Moench et al. 377).

But this journeyman period also puts him at a disadvantage historically, particularly when compared to someone like Jack Kirby. As Hatfield notes, the 1970s initiated a particularly uneven era for Kirby, one that "drove off all but loyalists" (13). That Kirby's lesser period coincides with the rise of Bronze Age artists like Pérez—who began work in comics in the mid-1970s—allows Pérez to be seen as part of a wave of artists coming to prominence as Kirby began to wane.

What commonly defines Kirby as an artist is work he did well into his overall career. Specifically, Kirby's greatest achievements in comic art stem from classic Marvel runs on *Fantastic Four* and

Thor as well as later works like *Eternals* and, at DC, his Fourth World books. However, by the start of *Fantastic Four*, Kirby had been working professionally in comics for well over twenty years, beginning with newspaper strips in 1936. But this journeyman period gets lopped off in the common conception of Kirby. As Hatfield notes, Kirby's earlier work on romance comics is "an open secret" whose "neglect . . . gives a distorted sense of Kirby's career" (22). With Pérez, however, the discussion of his contributions as an artist includes his most amateur efforts. If, for instance, Pérez and Kirby were compared at similar points in both their careers, the conversation about Pérez would start in the 1990s and with works like *Hulk: Future Imperfect* and his latter run on *Avengers*, both of which feature Pérez at one of his peaks.

However, this early work laid the groundwork for what Pérez would evolve into as an artist; for all its roughness, it exhibits some of what would become hallmarks of his style and thus his ability to "play with" what it is possible to do on the comic page. The first panel in *The Deadly Hands of Kung Fu* no. 6, in which Bob Diamond walks warily down the deserted corridors of a convention center, represents an early effort to embed characters and events within a larger storyworld. In particular, the walls to Diamond's left are papered with five posters, each advertising a different event at the center: closest to Diamond is one advertising the upcoming performance of the Ringling Bros. and Barnum & Bailey Circus; behind him and alongside a set of stairs are four more posters, each depicting a different event. Clearly discernible are a rodeo, a hockey game, and ice skating (Moench et al. 371). Later in the same issue, when the scene, as mentioned earlier, shifts to Diamond's home on page 7, we get a very detailed background (see figure 1.1). Books populate shelves in the far back, while an ornate lamp, what look like newspapers or magazines, and various other chotchkes are on Diamond's desk in front of him (Moench et al. 377). Here, again, is a clear sense of a world surrounding and thus inhabited by the characters, a signature aspect of Pérez's art that even this early work possesses.

These early issues similarly demonstrate ways in which Pérez "plays" with the configuration of the comic book page. Though Pérez sticks to various rectangular panels and pages in his first handful of issues, he does eventually vary some of his configurations. For example, in *The Deadly Hands of Kung Fu* no. 12, Pérez uses a triangular configuration on page 9 when Abe Brown, the black member of the Tigers that this issue spotlights, confronts plutonium smugglers. Pérez divides the bottom two-thirds of the page diagonally, with the top section featuring Brown delivering a leaping spread-eagled sidekick to his opponents' faces and the bottom depicting Brown slugging a third man (Moench et al. 740). With his first *Avengers* run, Pérez demonstrates some early use of vertically composed panels, such as on page 7 of issue 143 where Hawkeye, the Two-Gun Kid, Moondragon, and a disguised Thor suffer an energy blast from Kang; each appear in their own page-long vertical panel, positioned diagonally from top left to bottom right (Englehart et al. 350). Pérez's effort to deviate from the standard panel configuration pops up again in later *Avengers* issues, such as no. 168 during the confrontation between original Guardian of the Galaxy Starhawk and Michael Korvac; over the several pages of the battle, Pérez utilizes circular, vertical, triangular, and diagonal panels, the altered shape and configuration indicating the cosmic nature of their conflict, divorced—and thus differently composed—from the quotidian reality of the Marvel Universe (Shooter et al., *Korvac Saga* 70–74).

At this early stage, Pérez was also starting to construct the comics page to achieve other effects. An example of this comes in *The Deadly Hands of Kung Fu* no. 14, an issue shifting the spotlight to Lin Sun, the Chinese American member of the Tigers. In this story, Lin Sun's astral spirit travels back in time to team up with his samurai ancestor Kanbei Kikuchiyo against a group of bandits working for a personification of death. At one point in the plot, on page 8 of the story, Lin Sun witnesses the aftermath of the bandits' attack on a village (figure 1.2). To convey the horror of what Lin Sun sees, Pérez uses the middle tier of panels as a series

Figure 1.2. Lin Sun witnesses the horror of bandits' attack on a village from *Deadly Hands of Kung Fu*, no. 14, 1975 (Moench et al. 849).

of snapshots. Six identically vertical and rectangular panels each depict a different scene: a man lying dead from multiple arrows piercing his chest, a house burning above the corpse of another man with an arrow protruding from his back, a vulture picking at yet another body, a dead woman with blood dripping from an arrow in her chest and sprawled across what looks like a rooftop, a flock of vultures flying over burning parts of the village, and, finally, a vulture claw hovering above the hand of yet another corpse (Moench et al. 849). The horror effect derives from a time dilation this sequence achieves, aided by the panels framing it: in the page's first panel, Lin Sun asks, "Why, Ronin??" and the panel following the sequence has Lin Sun asking, again, "Why?" The entire sequence takes place within the pause between his statements, each of the six panels a beat occurring within that single beat.

Avengers no. 147 features a similar effort. On page 8 of the issue, two women sunbathe (panel 1). The next panel moves in closer on the pair, who are now partially covered by a shadowy form (panel 2), and the next pulls in closely on the red-headed sunbather's face completely in shadow (panel 3). Panel 4 pulls into just a shot of her shadowed eye behind sunglasses, and the final panel shifts to a perspective just behind the sunbathers who peer up at the Vision and Iron Man flying above them (Englehart et al. 426). Though the flight of the heroes and thus the shadowing of the women would have taken, at most, seconds, Pérez breaks the panel down into beats again happening within that moment, dilating and thus expanding the reader's experience of time. In talking about similar effects in *The New Teen Titans*, Harvey dismisses such efforts by Pérez as a "kind of visual gimmickry" and only "a neat visual trick" with "little narrative impact" (*The Art* 160). But as the example from *The Deadly Hands of Kung Fu* in particular demonstrates, Pérez, even at this early stage, was adept at manipulating the comic page and its effect to impact a narrative.

The potential exhibited in this early work was fully realized with the first watershed moment in Pérez's career: his departure from

Marvel for DC in 1980. Pérez identified several factors contributing to this shift. First, he enjoyed greater creative involvement at DC; *The New Teen Titans* was wholly his and Marv Wolfman's to play with and develop, unlike *Fantastic Four* and *Avengers* for which he was working with preexisting concepts and characters (Pérez and Biggers 80). Second, he found himself free of whatever strictures Marvel's "house style" imposed, allowing him to innovate on the page particularly in terms of building pages vertically and horizontally. This freedom also resulted from the greater involvement he felt as a creator; he notes that in his collaboration with Wolfman, the pair were able to plan stories that facilitated the use of vertical panels (Pérez and Biggers 84).

But beyond just stretching the page vertically, Pérez creates other spatial effects that speak to the power of his artwork and style. A case in point comes from the second issue of *Tales of the New Teen Titans* (1982), a series that expanded upon the origins of the three new characters created for the series (Cyborg, Raven, and Starfire) as well as Changeling, formerly known as Beast Boy in DC's *Doom Patrol* (1964) series. The second issue spotlights Raven and opens with a three-page nightmare sequence, in which she is tormented by and attempts to battle her demonic father, Trigon. The second page of this sequence comprises six narrow, vertical panels running from the top to the bottom of the page (figure 1.3). In the first two, Trigon shatters the rocks on which Raven stands, sending her plummeting through space in the third. She is caught by and kneels in the hand of her mother, Arella, in the fourth and fifth panels before her mother's visage is burned away to its skull and Raven begins her fall again (Wolfman et al. 1: 597). What is interesting to note about these panels is Raven's positioning in them: she remains in roughly the same place in each panel, just below the middle of the page. Thus, she is both falling and remaining still. Additionally, her positioning shifts and rotates in the panels. In the first, she kneels upright, while in the second, she is turned 180 degrees, falling headfirst. She continues to do so in the third panel before landing horizontally in her mother's

Figure 1.3. Raven's nightmare from *Tales of The New Teen Titans*, no. 2, 1982 (Wolfman et al. 1: 597).

hand in the fourth. Paralleling the first panel, Raven again kneels upright in the fifth, only to fall again when the hand disappears, and she again turns 180 degrees in the direction opposite to the previous panel. Overall, the effect here is that Raven is both falling and remaining in the same place while also spinning around and around, all of which contribute to how she feels at others' mercy.

A page from Pérez's *Wonder Woman* demonstrates another spatial effect he achieved. On page 6 of issue 7, Diana remains comatose and slowly dying following her defeat of Ares in the previous issue. She is thus pulled beneath the waters of Themyscira by the god Poseidon so that her life force can be restored, a process Pérez depicts over a series of six horizontal panels (figure 1.4). The panels also shrink further and further along this horizontal axis until the last two are inset within the page's final panel depicting Poseidon and his underwater grotto (Pérez et al., *Wonder Woman* 166). The overall effect is, again, twofold: there is a sense of both Diana moving lower and lower but also further and further back, owing to how her form necessarily shrinks along with the panels enclosing it. This second effect is enhanced by the black horizontal panels behind the ones depicting Diana, which, in the end, form the top of a cave-like entrance. Though the panels enclosing Diana are in front of these blackened panels to start, they and thus she are under the cave/grotto space they help to create in the final panel. In the end, the entire sequence works to create not only a sense of depth vertically, as Diana is pulled down, but also a sense of depth in that she is pulled backwards into the final panel at the bottom of the page.

A panel from page 3 of *Crisis on Infinite Earths* no. 7 demonstrates that the density of Bronze Age comics was no obstacle to the kinds of effects Pérez was able to achieve, even within a single panel (figure 1.5). This panel shifts the scene to Earth-2, home of DC's World War II–era heroes, most prominently the Justice Society and the All-Star Squadron. As a result of its positioning within the larger narrative of *Crisis*, there is a lot of information conveyed in this panel as it must establish the current state of Earth-2,

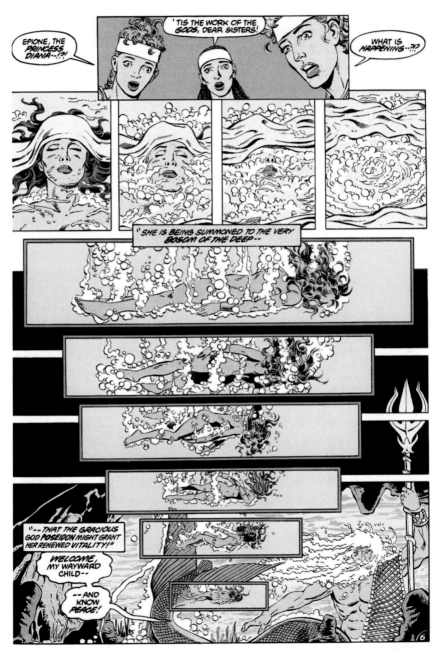

Figure 1.4. Diana/Wonder Woman's descent to Poseidon's grotto from *Wonder Woman*, vol. 2, no. 7, 1987 (Pérez et al., *Wonder Woman* 166).

Figure 1.5. Wildcat observes members of the All-Star Squadron from
Crisis on Infinite Earths, no. 7, 1985 (Wolfman and Pérez 177).

where multiple Earths are starting to merge, the presence of three
members of the All-Star Squadron (Green Arrow, the Atom, and
Liberty Belle), and the presence of the second-generation Wildcat, Yolanda Montez. To do so, Pérez divides the panel into three
sections. In the bottom left, he depicts how the different time
periods are merging on this Earth with a pterodactyl flying near
a traditional house that sits next to futuristic skyscrapers. In the
middle, the three Squadron members stand on what we will later

learn is a hospital roof while, in the top right, Wildcat peers down at them from what seems a much higher perch. In addition to the panel's density, its design and layout create a dizzying effect that reflects the various heights it conveys. The left-to-right motion of the panel takes the reader from ground level to the hospital roof to an even higher roof, where Yolanda watches. But the panel's perspective comes from a point above and behind Wildcat's/Yolanda's head, which is slightly above the middle of the panel and thus forms a kind of center around which it revolves. The entire effect is vertigo inducing, a trick added to by the forced perspective Pérez uses in the panel, as the first panel on the next page reveals that Yolanda actually is not as high up in comparison to the other three heroes as she appears here (Wolfman and Pérez 177–78). Though this page, like the others discussed above, are discrete examples of Pérez's work as a comic artist, cumulatively they testify to certain ways he "plays" with and within the dimensions of the comic page and panel, contributions to the composition of comics art that have been unduly underrated.

These stylistic effects that Pérez achieved on the comic book page are only one part of his artistic legacy, however. Another and perhaps larger aspect of his significance as a comic book artist lies in his construction of comic book storyworlds. Just as he stretches physical possibilities on the page, Pérez exploits the possibilities inherent within the visual realization of the world surrounding his characters and events. Furthermore, in doing so, Pérez expresses and, more importantly, embraces a sense of the fantastic that inheres within comic book storyworlds, particularly those based in superhero fantasy.

A "storyworld" is precisely what its name implies: it is the "world" (or, as is often the case, "worlds") conjured up by the "story," by a narrative.[4] In *Story Logic* (2002), Brian Herman discusses, as a particular feature of narrative, how it moves readers between worlds: from a present-day world of person-to-person interaction to the "world" of a reader encountering a text/narrative—be it in print, film, or other media—and, finally, to the world within that text/

narrative (14). In other words, a feature of narrative is its ability to remove or "de-center" readers from the actual world in which they encounter a narrative text and emplace or "re-center" them within the world/worlds that narrative text imagines and thus constructs. As Herman goes on to say, "*all* storytellers cue their audiences to transport themselves from the spatiotemporal parameters of the current interaction to those defining the storyworld" (271, emphasis original). "The Prologue" in Geoffrey Chaucer's *The Canterbury Tales* (c. 1387), Herman explains, shifts readers to the world in which the characters' pilgrimage occurs and, from there, to the worlds within each of the various pilgrim's tales (272). Similarly, he asserts that Joseph Conrad's *Heart of Darkness* (1899) requires the reader to make multiple relocations, again from their world in which they are encountering the physical text to that in which Marlowe tells his story and thus to the storyworld embedded within that telling (272–73). To not do so in either case (or similar ones) impedes understanding and thus interpretation.

Herman goes on to assert how interpretation of narrative hinges upon discerning between what is real or actual within those storyworlds versus what is perceived or imagined by persons within them (15). Thus, the storyworld has an objective status separate from its inhabitants' subjective perceptions of it. In *Heterocosmica* (1998), Lubomír Doležel echoes Herman on the nature of storyworlds as different and independent from the world of the real/actual, and thus they and how they function have to be discerned (16, 19). Such fictional worlds are again created by authors and subsequently processed and reconstructed by readers. How a text and its constructed storyworld are processed thus hinges upon various aspects of the reader: their purpose, their skills, their style of reading, etc. (21). But this adds an implicit sense of possibility inhering within storyworlds that is particularly relevant for comics. For instance, Doležel sees how these fictional worlds are incomplete and heterogeneous as essential to how they function. Only certain things are known (or "decidable" to use Doložel's term) within texts while others are not. He cites examples such as the cause of

Emma Bovary's death in Gustave Flaubert's *Madame Bovary* (1856) and the number of children Lady Macbeth had in Shakespeare's *Macbeth* (1623) as things known/decidable and not, respectively (22). However, in being so incomplete, narrative storyworlds are almost an enticement to completion.

This urge to fill in these gaps speaks to the kind of narrative continuity, retconning, and fan fiction that have become commonplace if not cottage industries within and around superhero comics. Marvel, for example, used to give out No Prizes to fans who both caught and then explained away gaffes in their continuity; thus, a kind of incompleteness—an error—invited a reader to proffer an explanation for why it was not an error, thus rendering the storyworld once again, in a way, "whole" or "complete." What Doležel describes as the heterogeneous nature of narrative storyworlds also feeds into the possibility inherent within comic narratives, including those of superhero fantasy.

Pérez's work in comics is an embrace of these functions and possibilities inherent within comic book storyworlds. The earlier examples of the convention center and Diamond's home in *The Deadly Hands of Kung Fu* testify to this aspect of his work from its start, and it would only become more definitive as his career advanced. Pérez singles out the splash page of *Avengers* no. 167—the first issue of the Korvac Saga—as representative of how his work had evolved to that point (figure 1.6). He specifically cites the background filled with machinery and the wash of detail as aspects that make it so, aspects that are part of the storyworld around the characters (Baker 28–29).

However, previous issues reveal Pérez's tendency toward storyworld building existing even earlier than this exemplar issue. *Avengers* no. 154, in which the team confronts the Atlantean villain Tyrak within Avengers Mansion, provides multiple opportunities for Pérez to hint at the larger world and history around the characters. Two panels at the top of page 5 illustrate the Scarlet Witch walking through the halls of the mansion and into an exterior garden; both images are particularly ornate in the mansion's details,

Figure 1.6. Splash page from *Avengers*, vol. 1, no. 167, 1977 (Shooter et al., *Korvac Saga* 42).

particularly the latter one, in which Pérez lavishes attention to both the mansion interior and outdoor garden. Once the battle begins, Pérez still sneaks what might seem extraneous details into scenes that actually speak to the history of the team. On page 15, for instance, as Captain America swings his shield into Tyrak's chest, portraits of the Hulk and Hawkeye hang on the wall behind the battle. And, on page 16, as Tyrak knocks a wall down on the assembled heroes, pictures of Howard and Maria Stark—Iron Man/Tony Stark's parents, whose mansion the team occupies—fall among the rubble (Shooter et al., *Final Threat* 119, 129, 130). This was one way in which Pérez's style developed as he continued to work in comics.

Another feature of Pérez's storyworlds places him squarely in continuity with Kirby. Hatfield, working from Leo Marx and several other scholars, characterizes the presence of what he terms the "technological sublime" in Kirby's work. In this, Hatfield links Kirby with an experience of the sublime that is ambivalent, provoking not only a sense of awe and wonder but also darker feelings of "shock, estrangement, and madness" (145–46). Singer, too, recognizes the presence of this "technological sublime" in Pérez's work, connecting what he terms a "fusion of the diagrammatic and dramatic" in a page from Cyborg's origin in *Tales of the New Teen Titans* no. 1 to similar feelings of "awe and fear" ("George Pérez" 295). But while this moment conveys this contrasting duet of response, what more often results from the level of detail Pérez puts into the storyworlds is a sense of the sublime akin to solely an awestruck wonder. Like with Kirby, it can often be found in representations of technology. Part of what causes Pérez's evocation of the technological sublime to differ from Kirby's is its placement within the storyworld surrounding the characters, as opposed to something distinct, anomalous, and thus fear inducing. There is, for instance, a kind of wonder evoked by the way in which Pérez surrounds his characters and thus builds into their worlds this kind of wondrous technology. Though the exterior of Pérez's Avengers Mansion might look like any other

Fifth Avenue edifice, the interior, such as seen in issue 160, is full of technological marvels. The fifth panel on page 4, which reveals the team's attacker as the Grim Reaper, brother to the recently resurrected Wonder Man, is a good example of this pattern. The Grim Reaper stands on a hyperdetailed cylinder while banks of other computerized wonders stand floor to ceiling behind him (Shooter et al., *Final Threat* 244). The splash page to *Avengers* no. 167 (see figure 1.6) that Pérez singled out as representative of his work on this era of the title likewise evokes this alternative sense of a technological sublime. In this image, the Beast, the Scarlet Witch, and Captain America respond to an alarm. Surrounding them—in both the foreground and background—are more of the same kind of hyperdetailed computer banks and other wonder tech that again run from floor to ceiling. The first panel on the next page continues this evocation, as the trio enter the Avengers' cavernous communications room that, too, is a technological wonder. And then, on the third page, the top half depicts a screen image of a massive satellite construct above Earth, dwarfing the S.H.I.E.L.D. orbital platform, an image that prompts from Cap an awestruck "God, mother and country . . . It . . . It's awesome!" (Shooter et al., *Korvac Saga* 42–44).

But Pérez does not limit such evocation of a sublime wonder to just the technological artifacts of his storyworlds. It is part and parcel of those worlds' built environments. In his chapter on superheroes and the city in *Matters of Gravity*, Scott Bukatman describes the city as twofold in its nature, represented, to use his terms, by the concepts of "the grid" and "grace." The "grid" evokes the city as a "rational system," as ordered and structured, represented in its topographical map of streets and avenues (Bukatman 186–87). Simultaneously, however, these grids also give license to locales within them that are less "rational," less "ordered" and thus chaotic and even utopian. Within the city itself, such "grace" is embodied both in its skyscrapers—"the upward thrust of the city, . . . every separate floor and room defined by its own unique and grandiose designs and imaginings" (186)—and spaces like the

Roman Gardens that "represent [an] ideal world removed in time and space" and "supplant the utilitarian'" (qtd. on 186).

Pérez's art is a clear distillation of the "grid" and "grace" that Bukatman describes, and the sense of the sublime that art conveys derives from these contrasting traits. The first page of *The New Teen Titans* preview in *DC Comics Presents* no. 26 is a clear example of how Pérez expresses the dual-natured city. Filling the background of the image are skyscrapers of various heights, a brick-and-mortar building on the left, and, to the right, a series of skyscrapers, increasing in height toward the edge of the page. Here, we might see represented the "upward thrust" Bukatman associated with such buildings and thus the grandiose possibilities within the city. But it is the center of this image that takes what Bukatman describes about the city a step further. There, Pérez places the S.T.A.R. Labs building. The front and back walls of the building are sloped so that the building narrows in the middle before sloping back out slightly, giving it a rounded trapezoidal shape. This contrasts the surrounding buildings, all perfectly rectangular. Further contrasting the S.T.A.R. building is its front, nearly entirely windowed, which stands in marked contrast to the rest of its surrounding cityscape. In this, it also contrasts the regularity of those other skyscrapers, which, if those others can also be said to express the grace and sublimity of the city, the contrasting design of S.T.A.R. Labs must also do and perhaps to an even greater extent (Wolfman et al. 1: 12).

But if this opening image of S.T.A.R. Labs captures the sublime grace and wonder inherent in Pérez's comic book worlds, another building he would soon design does so to an even greater extent. In *The New Teen Titans* no. 3, the team was gifted what would become their new headquarters: Titans Tower, a T-shaped building located in the East River adjacent to Manhattan. Issue 7 unveils the full nature of this architectural wonder as Cyborg finds the blueprints for the building, which Pérez then drew for readers to see on page 9 (figure 1.7) of the issue (Wolfman et al. 1: 191). Such schematics are, as Bukatman points out, commonplace within

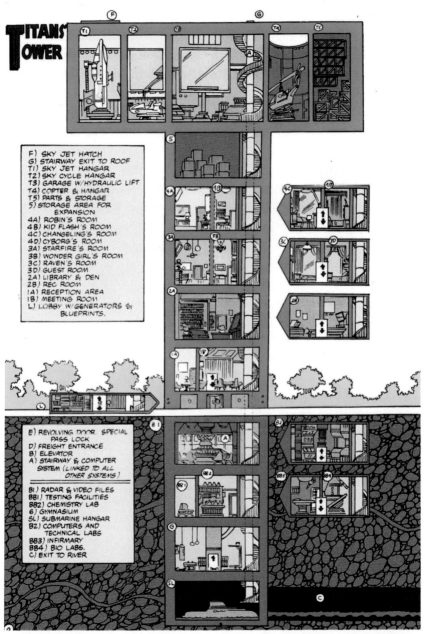

Figure 1.7. The blueprint of Titans Tower from *The New Teen Titans*, vol. 1, no. 7, 1981 (Wolfman et al. 1: 191).

superhero comics, as he uses the diagram of the Fantastic Four's Baxter Building to illustrate. They are also an embodiment of the dual nature of skyscrapers/the city, as they simultaneously represent them as "both rational and fantastic spaces" (Bukatman 191). As schematics, they are inherently rational. Titans Tower, as the image shows, is divided into three levels: above ground, there are the two parts of the T, the horizontal, uppermost level and the vertical column, each of which are composed of various rooms/ spaces; below ground, the vertical column continues as a series of basement levels, ending in an exit via the East River. Further adding to the rational nature of this tower is how the various interior spaces are labeled according to their location: the topmost level is comprised of rooms T1 through T5; the aboveground part of the columnar section is marked, starting from the top, as floors five through one before ending in the tower's lobby; and then the various basement levels are labeled as B1 and B2, BB1 through BB4, G (for "gymnasium"), and, finally, SL for the "submarine hangar" that feeds into the exit. And the spaces are consistently rectangular, the ones in the columnar section appearing pretty much uniform in their dimensions.

Coexisting with this obvious rationality is the equally apparent fantastic dimension to Titans Tower. Like Kirby's design plan for the Baxter Building, various spaces within Titans Tower speak to the fantastic, the exuberant, and thus a kind of the sublime. In addition to expected spaces, such as private rooms for each of the Titans, various storage spaces, a library, and a den, there are rooms serving as hangars for the Titans' "Sky Jet" and "Sky Cycles" as well as a helicopter. Below ground, behind a "revolving door" with a "special pass lock," Titans Tower contains rooms for "radar" and "video files," a "chemistry lab," "computers and technical labs," an infirmary, and "bio labs." But surpassing all of this is the nature of the very building itself. Its T-shape is, frankly, ridiculous. One can only wonder how it manages to stay up, particularly when the hangars for the jet and cycles are in the spaces furthest to the left on the top/horizontal level. Given the additional and significant tons of weight to one side of the building, the fact that this unbalanced structure does not topple over to one side is extraordinary.

The wonder inherent in such a building as Titans Tower permeates even less prominent locations Pérez designed. *The New Teen Titans* no. 3 introduces the villain team the Fearsome Five and their original headquarters. Sibling villains Mammoth and Shimmer arrive at an unassuming location to meet with the rest of their compatriots, the original Dr. Light, the telepathic Psimon, and the inventive Gizmo. On page 4 of the issue, the Five first gather in a meeting room filled with green marbled columns and archways, all quite ornately decorated. On page 8, they walk just above another columned archway on a cobblestone floor; on the wall behind them are several arched windows as well as various bulbous lamps and other details (Wolfman et al. 1: 82, 86). Most crucial about this image is the way in which the characters within it are dwarfed by these surroundings. The figures are actually a very small part of this image, literally occupying only the bottom half of the panel. The effect is to convey a sense of how encompassed they are by their environment, one that is depicted with an extraordinary level of detail and thus speaks to not so much a conventional realism but a more exaggerated and ultimately sublime reality that they inhabit.

The expression of these two forms of the sublime—the technological and environmental that Pérez builds into his storyworlds—is to be found in his later work as well. They come together, for example, in *Avengers* no. 20 from his run with Busiek. This issue is the second part of their celebrated "Ultron Unlimited" arc and begins with the assembled team meeting with US military leaders. The first page contains a total of eight panels focusing on the Avengers' arrival at the Pentagon. Various moments crystallize over this sequence of panels: Justice and Firestar's whispered conversation regarding Black Panther's status with the team in panels 3 and 5, Captain America's steely eyed glance at the Panther in panel 4, Cap's chastisement of Justice and Firestar in 6 and 7, and, in both panels 4 and 8, the Panther's stoic silence. The left-hand side of the following two-page splash continues this pattern, as Justice and Firestar continue their conversation and then are interrupted and counseled by Thor. This sequence culminates in the roughly page-and-a-half splash/title page, which depicts the Avengers' arrival at the Pentagon's command center (figure 1.8). It is this final image where the two forms of the sublime function simultaneously. On the one hand, the Pentagon command center is clearly a technological wonder. It gleams in various shades of metallic gray, and Pentagon workers sit at various computer banks/ workstations. On the other hand, this setting dwarfs the Avengers themselves as they are positioned at the lowest level of the center and so—not unlike the Fearsome Five in their headquarters but to a much, much greater extent—engulfed by what surrounds them. The way in which the series of smaller, almost cramped panels on the preceding page and first quarter of this two-page splash create a kind of claustrophobic experience add to the effect of the larger image, as it literally opens the scene up to a much wider and wondrous representation of this locale.[5]

Costume design is another place where Pérez embraces this sense of the sublime, costuming being another part of what Bukatman describes as the "hyperbolic spectacle" of comics (186). In this, Pérez differs from a trend that would develop in the early twenty-first century. A case in point comes from Fox's *X-Men* (2000). As Hugh Jackman's Wolverine chafes against the black leather costumes the team wears, asking, "You actually go outside in these things?" James Marsden's Cyclops quips back, "Well, what would you prefer? Yellow spandex?" (*X-Men*). This exchange is built on an explicit contrast between the greater realism and practicality attached to the film X-Men's black leather attire and the ridiculous and outré nature of traditional superhero costumes. The comics the film was based on soon followed suit. In their manifesto pitching their ideas for the *New X-Men* title, which launched in 2001, writer Grant Morrison wrote, "GET RID OF THE COSTUMES. Let's ditch the spandex for the new century and get our heroes into something that wouldn't make you look like a [redacted] if you wore it in the

Figure 1.8. The Pentagon's command center from *Avengers*, vol. 3, no. 20, 1999 (Busiek and Pérez 1: n.p.).

street" (2, emphasis and redaction original). Describing their new look as "brutalist and military," Morrison eschewed the bright "pop art dayglo" colors of the comic book past, except as "panelling or detailing" and explicitly links their effort with that of the 2000 film (2). With both, though, comes a kind of tapping down of the fantastical, extraordinary, hyperbolic aspects of superhero comics into a more muted, realist aesthetic.

In contrast, the "performative flamboyance" that Bukatman argues connects superhero costumes to the circus is very much on display in many of Pérez's designs (214–15). Probably the first one that comes to mind is Starfire of the New Teen Titans, whose original costume would not be out of place on the streets of Rio during Carnival. Expressing a different kind of flamboyance in costuming is the Avenger the Wasp, who has a long history of donning different costumes, which Pérez certainly contributed to. Though the Wasp appeared in a costume that was simply a red swimsuit over a blue leotard for much of Pérez's early run on *Avengers*, with issue 161, he started varying her costume, beginning with a sleeveless purple jumpsuit with cutouts around her stomach and waist as well as running down both legs. In no. 167, at her own fashion show, the Wasp donned an all-white two-piece ensemble with a draped top and skirt. In issue 170, as the team once again faces Ultron, the Wasp donned yet another new outfit, pairing gold thigh-high boots with a gold swimsuit top, with various W-shaped trim around a plunging collar and boot tops. With *Avengers* no. 194, Pérez created one of the Wasp's best-known costumes, a white unitard with blue trimming and a diagonal design that exposed her left leg and right arm.

But Pérez's flamboyant costume designs were not reserved for his female characters (figure 1.9). He famously designed Dick Grayson's first costume as Nightwing, combining shades of dark and light blue with yellow highlights and a popped collar that feeds into an open neck plunging to his mid chest. That same issue—*Tales of the Teen Titans* no. 44—also debuted the future Titan Jericho's costume: a white turtleneck under an ornate vest in purple and gold, blue leggings, and purple boots with golden cuffs. Male villains designed by Pérez have similarly flamboyant outfits. Deathstroke, a master assassin, wears an outfit inexplicably combining dark blue with orange buccaneer boots, shorts, gloves, and the left side of his mask. Marvel's Taskmaster, who debuted in *Avengers* no. 195, has perhaps an even more ludicrous-seeming outfit, particularly given the secretive nature of his original motivation. As the to-this-point hidden supplier of generic thugs to supervillains, one might expect Taskmaster to have a more muted appearance. Instead, he sports a blue-and-orange color palette not unlike Deathstroke's but adds bright-white buccaneer boots, shorts, gloves, and a hood and mask along with a massive and flowing cape. Inherent within all these characters—heroes and

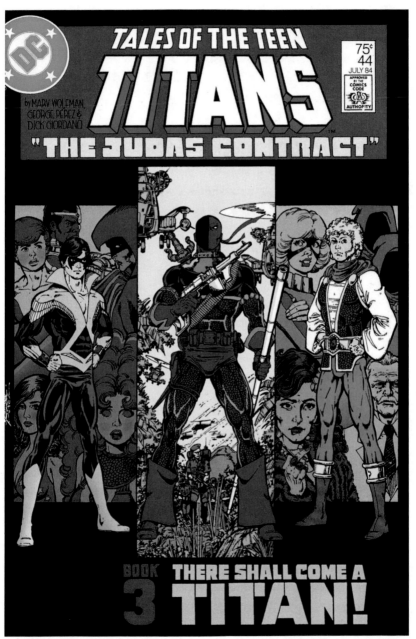

Figure 1.9. The cover of *Tales of the Teen Titans*, vol. 1, no. 44, 1984 (Wolfman et al. 3: 59).

villains, male and female—is the kind of "audacious performance" that "slip[s] the bonds of conventional behavior" summed up by Bukatman (217). It is also again another example of the ways in which Pérez eschews a kind of conventional realism within superhero comics' representation of their storyworlds and those who inhabit it.

All these traits in Pérez's work—storyworld building, a sense of the sublime, an embracing of the fantastic and hyperbolic inherent in comics—come together in a moment from one of his most acclaimed works (figure 1.10): *Hulk: Future Imperfect*, published in 1992 and written by long-time Hulk scribe Peter David. In the first issue of this two-part event series, Hulk is brought by Janis Jones, the granddaughter of Rick Jones, Hulk's original teenage sidekick, to the dystopic future run by the despotic Maestro, a future version of the Hulk himself. He reunites with an aged and deteriorating Rick Jones in a room filled with relics of Marvel superheroes and villains (David et al. 270–71).

Tellingly, David's script called for only a handful of items—the surfboard of the Silver Surfer, Captain America's shield, Wolverine's adamantium skeleton, and a shelf of jars containing the cremains of various heroes and villains—while the rest was left to Pérez's imagination (Lawrence 90). Typical of Pérez, he went far beyond what was expected. Across the ceiling, alongside a broken remnant of the Surfer's board, hang the helmets of Thor, the second Yellowjacket, Sunfire, the Black Knight, the Crimson Dynamo, Magneto, the Wizard, Nova, Ant-Man, Ultron, and the first Titanium Man, as well as Spider-Man's black costume. Various capes also hang from the rafters of the room; recognizable ones include Thor's, Quasar's, Dr. Doom's, the Scarlet Witch's, and Cloak's. In the far back of the first page hangs a dilapidated Fantasti-Car, once transportation for the Fantastic Four. Around the room are various other relics. Some are clearly enshrined: a collection of various Iron Man helmets and chest plates (behind which looms what appears to be the green Power Battery of Oa belonging to DC's Green Lantern); Dr. Strange's Cloak of Levitation and Eye of

Figure 1.10. Future Rick Jones's trophy room from *Hulk: Future Imperfect*, no. 1, 1992 (David et al. 270–71).

Agamotto (below a picture of Shatterstar next to one of his two double-bladed swords and a trident that could be either Namor's or, more likely, the Son of Satan's, though it doesn't quite match either); Spider-Man's mask and web shooter; Thor's Mjolnir; Dr. Doom's faceplate held aloft by a mechanical arm; Professor X's original wheelchair (Rick Jones currently occupies his high-tech, floating version); the heads of Vision and the New Mutants' Warlock below what are likely fragments of the Black Knight's Ebony Blade and next to the blue-furred pelt of the X-Men's Beast; Daredevil's collapsing billy club/cane; Wolverine's adamantium skeleton, complete with claws; Captain America's mask and shield above a picture of the original Captain Marvel and U.S. Agent's mask and broken shield; a picture of Cap and Bucky; and part of Hawkeye's bow alongside a quiver and his various trick arrows.

Other items appear scattered more haphazardly around the room: Cyclops's visor sits in the bottom left corner on a table or desk; in the bottom right corner are the mechanical legs of Stilt-Man and the mechanical arms of Dr. Octopus, a wrecking ball, presumably once belonging to the Absorbing Man, and, in a nod to Pérez's own past, the jade necklace of the White Tiger. Near these sits a Sentinel head covered in debris and, a little further back, the second Ghost Rider's motorcycle. On shelves in the far back can be seen a red skull (possibly that of the Red Skull) and the Serpent Crown (not to mention the Bottle City of Kandor, another item from the DC rather than the Marvel Universe).

The significance of the image Pérez creates on these two pages, however, goes beyond providing astute comic book fans a satisfying hunt for obvious and obscure "Easter eggs." The various relics conglomerated in this display are themselves the detritus of the storyworld they serve to incarnate. That is, there is clearly a sense of a world having been built and thus being represented here. Ruth Ronen speaks to this in her discussion of storyworlds and "possible worlds" in fiction. She writes, "a world of fiction constitutes a discrete system with a modal structure of its own," continuing on to describe how such a world "connotes a whole complex of states of affairs. . . . A fictional world, like any possible world, is analogous to the actual world in that it has its own set of facts and its own subworlds and counter-worlds" (Ronen 29). The various items all speak to "facts" and various "sub-worlds"—those of the Avengers family of heroes/titles, the X-Men, and other Marvel heroes, for example—that exist within the Marvel Universe proper. Though Pérez can hardly be described as the only creator responsible for "building" this world, his art on this page invokes it via a kind of metonymy where each piece in the display (for example, Spider-Man's and Dr. Doom's masks) not only substitutes itself for that of which it is part (Spider-Man, Dr. Doom) but also the larger history behind those characters (i.e., Spider-Man's history as represented in his family of titles, Dr. Doom being a part of the *Fantastic Four*, whose history is invoked elsewhere as well by items like the Fantasti-Car). In this, then, we can see the way in which Pérez as a comics creator very much thinks of his work as taking place in and helping contribute to a larger world that surrounds the characters and that into which readers are invited.

But there are other effects achieved here as well. For one, there is a sense of narrative. In general, the collection of these relics indicates both the end of what we might think of as the "Age of Heroes" and the end of the individual heroes themselves. And some of those individual ends are given at least some pathos: Wolverine's skeleton and, perhaps most pointedly, the Beast's pelt, which would have required the hirsute hero to be skinned at some point, are particularly horrific. There, too, appear to be even subtle in-jokes in some of the images. A poster on the back wall clearly presents a figure surrounded by the Phoenix force with a caption at the top reading "DEAD . . . AGAIN!" playing on this presence/character's tendency toward resurrection. Similarly, the intact and pristine state of Captain America's shield hanging above the broken and haphazardly leaned remnant of U.S. Agent's is a visual slur at the Agent's lesser standing as a hero and failure as a stand-in Captain. There is, furthermore, that sense of the sublime and wonder in this image. David underlines this in the script via a stunned Hulk's dialogue in the two connected dialogue balloons: "Oh" followed by "My Lord" that echoes Captain America's stunned wonder at the Guardians' ship from back in *Avengers* no. 167. But even without this indication in the script, the image itself conveys a sense of awe and wonder in the sheer number of relics and thus nods to the comic book past, a kind of maximalization that is another hallmark of Pérez's art and thus what he contributed to comics both in terms of style and storytelling.

CHAPTER TWO

Overcoming Narratives of
Race and Disability

The invisibility Pérez suffers from as a comic book artist parallels a similar neglect of his work in cultural analyses of comics. Just as the nature of his art—its transparency as well as the various conditions that fostered that transparency—has tended to diminish his contributions to the visual aspects of comic book storytelling, so too have factors worked to the detriment of seeing Pérez as a creator who contributes to how comics participate in cultural narratives. Pérez's runs on mainstay titles like *Avengers*, *The New Teen Titans*, and *Wonder Woman* mean the bulk of his work focused on predominantly white and able-bodied characters. Historically, nonwhites and disability have played limited roles in such fare, and this fact similarly limits what Pérez might be seen and said to have done regarding their representation. In *The Deadly Hands of Kung Fu*, given the greater racial diversity of its cast, Pérez made more direct contributions to representations of racial difference; however, it is a more obscure title featuring characters largely marginalized within the Marvel pantheon of heroes.

Further complicating Pérez's position within those racial narratives is the mixed perception of his own status as a Latinx creator. Javier Hernandez, creator of *El Muerto: The Aztec Zombie*, in talking about what constitutes "a Latino comic book," questions Pérez's inclusion in this category, defining such creators as those who "create a story that's Latino-themed" (qtd. in Aldama, *Your Brain* 200). Hernandez even identifies Anglo writer and artist Jessica Abel as a more Latinx creator than Pérez (200). At the same time, there are Latinx creators who give Pérez greater credit.

Bobby Rubio, a freelance comics artist and Pixar Animation story artist, cites Pérez as his favorite artist growing up and celebrates "his facial expressions and his dynamic artwork" (qtd. on 258). And Aldama further redresses such blinkered appraisals of Pérez, citing him as the "most significant creator" of comics' Bronze Age (*Latinx Superheroes* 18).

Further muddying Pérez's contributions is the earlier-cited tendency to privilege writers over artists in much of comics history and scholarship. That it is necessary, for example, for Aldama to assert that art is just as significant as the plot and script in making Latinx superheroes successful suggests again how verbal has outweighed visual narrative making (*Latinx Superheroes* 4). However, this friction between the verbal and visual dimensions of comics further informs how Pérez contributes to these various discourses, particularly those related to race and disability, which this chapter discusses. In his largely (though not exclusively) visual constructions of characters, Pérez can be seen as subtly working to contradict problematic representations that at times persist within the plot and/or script. Regarding race, such characters include the Sons of the Tiger and the original White Tiger, Cyborg, and Triathlon; in the case of disability, Pérez's efforts largely hinge on Cyborg and Jericho of the New Teen Titans.

From Tigers to Triathlon:
Pérez and Narratives of Racial Difference

The Sons of the Tiger debuted as the final feature in *The Deadly Hands of Kung Fu* no. 1. There, after fending off a trio of ninja assassins, Chinese martial arts student Lin Sun watches his Master Kee die in his arms, an earlier victim of the ninjas. Kee gifts Lin with a jade tiger necklace, which he will share with two other of Kee's best students, the African American Abe Brown and the white actor Bob Diamond, to become the "Sons of the Tiger." The Sons are, thus, an early example of a multicultural super team and a rare one (in the mid-1970s) in that nonwhite members outnumber the white. Pérez took over as pencil artist on the Sons of the Tiger feature with issue 6 and handled those duties (for all but one issue) until no. 17 of the title.

Pérez's efforts on the series support its implicit multicultural messaging. Pérez's depictions of the Sons often speak to an equality that exists among the trio and thus, symbolically, embodies the equality such multicultural teams were meant to promote. In this, Pérez demonstrates what Aldama terms "geometrizing," "the skillful and willful visualizing . . . of character, theme, and plot" in comics (*Latinx Superheroes* 94). Being a trio, the three lend themselves to a very literal kind of geometrizing, which is to appear in triangular/tripartite arrangements. In issue 7's story "Tigers in a Mind Cage!," for example, the three Sons individually face their various inner demons (Diamond's own ego, Brown's childhood mugging, and Lin's own fears of failure). The final panel on page 10 of this story depicts all three breaking out of their respective "mind cages" at the same time and thus equally. Further underlining this equality are various other similarities that exist in Pérez's visualization of this moment: each bursts out through an equally sized concrete door, each does so via a single-legged kick, and each is centered behind the bursting rubble (Moench et al. 468). Pérez also, at times, geometrizes a thematic unity between the three disparate members of the Sons. Most obvious among these moments is when the Sons clasp hands and recite the oath that activates their abilities. In issue 6, for instance, this happens on page 14 as Brown and Diamond stand to either side of Lin, who is prostrate on the ground after being knifed in the back; a similar moment occurs on page 12 in issue 11, where Pérez arranges the trio triangularly in the foreground while a glowing tiger head floats behind them (384, 689). But there are also moments absent their oath when Pérez spatially represents a unity and coherence among the members of this multicultural trio. On page 10 of issue 8's "Storm of Vengeance," they combine to take out a sniper, Lin and Brown on the left and in front of the target, delivering kicks to his head and legs respectively while Diamond flies in from the right with a kick to the assailant's back (519).

In issue 19, the Sons of the Tiger disbanded because of internal conflicts, discarding the three parts of the jade tiger necklace that gave them enhanced abilities. This necklace would be found in the very same issue by Nuyorican Hector Ayala, who would don it and become Marvel's first Latinx superhero, the White Tiger. White Tiger would feature as the new lead of the Sons of the Tiger series through issue 32 (and *The Deadly Hands of Kung Fu* ended with no. 33); however, Pérez drew only a small handful of his appearances, in issues 19 through 21 and then issue 30.

The similarly Puerto Rican Pérez has been seen as having an intrinsic connection to White Tiger. However, the reality is not that straight forward and not just because of the limited time Pérez spent as the Tiger's primary artist. For one, Pérez credits the idea of creating Marvel's first Puerto Rican hero to writer Bill Mantlo more than himself. As Pérez relates in an interview with Heidi MacDonald, Mantlo was inspired by Pérez's background but also motivated by being profoundly "socially and politically conscious," using Pérez more as an informational source (MacDonald 11). Pérez goes further in a separate interview, not only explicitly stating that Ayala/White Tiger was Mantlo's idea, "not mine," but also that his then wife Yvie, not Pérez, worked with Mantlo on making the Spanish use in the series authentic (Nolen-Weathington 18).

What Pérez can take credit for are his efforts to position White Tiger more equally within the Marvel pantheon of heroes. Significant to this positioning are the ways in which White Tiger/Ayala functions in parallel to Spider-Man/Peter Parker. David Yurkovich outlines the numerous similarities between the two characters. White Tiger's costume was designed as a scaled-back version of Spidey's. Hector gets his powers through a not dissimilar chance encounter: he stumbles upon the Sons' discarded jade tiger necklace as opposed to Parker's radioactive spider-bite, but both plots depend on their soon-to-be heroes being in the right place at the right time to become empowered. Other similarities between the two quickly accrue: both are students at Empire State University in New York, both fight organized crime, and both are (wrongly) accused of being criminals themselves. Also, members of Peter Parker/Spider-Man's supporting cast find their way into White Tiger's adventures (Yurkovich 13).

But what, at least in part, keeps Ayala/White Tiger from seeming little more than a knockoff of Marvel's most popular hero is Pérez's visual depiction of him. Aldama identifies and analyzes some of the ways in which the artist distinguishes his new hero; he focuses on two particular images—Hector's initial transformation into the White Tiger at the end of *The Deadly Hands of Kung Fu* no. 19 and the splash page of his second appearance in no. 20—to explain the ways in which Pérez instills a strength and vibrancy to this character. Aldama adds White Tiger's first action sequence over pages 5–7 of this second appearance to the examples of how Pérez conveys an intensity and power to Ayala's character and movement (*Latinx Superheroes* 17–20). But White Tiger, under Pérez's pen, does not only demonstrate this forcefulness and power against nameless thugs. In his third appearance, "To Claw the Eyes of Night!" in *The Deadly Hands of Kung Fu* no. 21, White Tiger finds himself pursued not only by the police but by reformed Spider-Man villain the Prowler (a.k.a. Hobie Brown). Pérez's composition of their initial battle very much portrays the neophyte White Tiger—here in what is his very first battle with another costumed adventurer—as holding his own and thus implicitly on par with Spider-Man. A two-page spread on pages 13–14 is a particularly evocative example. Most striking is the diagonal panel that runs from the bottom left of the first page to the top right of the second, taking up the majority of the spread. It complementarily positions White Tiger and Prowler, the former launching up from the bottom of the panel to hurl a kick with his left leg at the latter while Prowler, his right leg almost perfectly symmetrical with Tiger's, falls back toward the top of the second panel. Continuing throughout Pérez's choreographing of this fight is a constant back and forth between the two that likewise speaks to

Figure 2.1. White Tiger battles the Prowler from *Deadly Hands of Kung Fu*, no. 21, 1976 (Claremont et al. 208).

a balance not only between them but, because of Prowler's origins in *Amazing Spider-Man*, also White Tiger and Marvel's arachnid hero. For example, in the second set of triangular panels that fill the bottom right corner of this spread, Prowler knocks a piece of brick rubble at Tiger, which, in the subsequent panel, he obliterates with a single punch (Claremont et al. 204–5).

Pérez similarly uses two different tripartite images to further underline White Tiger's equal abilities. The first comes on page 15 of the story, where, in a vertical column, Pérez presents three different instances of White Tiger and Prowler fighting hand to hand. Here, Tiger blocks Prowler's blow with his fist, then kicks him in his face before, in the final image, Prowler punches Tiger back, flipping him head over heels. This is then followed up on page 17 with a horizontal panel at the bottom where the Tiger is triumphant (figure 2.1): he punches Prowler in the chest with his left fist, then, in the second image, elbows him in the back of the head and down toward the ground with his right before, in the third and final image, kneeing Prowler in the chest, sending him flying backwards (Claremont et al. 206, 208). In both these instances, we see White Tiger holding his own against Prowler. Likewise, there is a strength and dominance—particularly in the second such image that feeds into the resolution of their battle— that, like those images Aldama explicates, firmly establish White Tiger as a powerful and dynamic presence.

After this three-issue introduction of White Tiger, Pérez only provides art for one more issue of the White Tiger/Sons of the Tiger feature in *The Deadly Hands of Kung Fu*, and that is not until issue 30. Pérez once again depicts White Tiger/Ayala in similarly powerful terms, particularly as he confronts a gang that invades his family's home, threatening both his sister and brother. In various panels—White Tiger kicking a thug into a pole while grappling another from behind (page 11, panel 2), kicking another thug headfirst into a glass window (page 12, panel 6), lifting yet another above his head in preparation to hurl him to the ground (page 13, panel 5)—Pérez draws a highly muscled form, which, in addition to the Tiger's actions, communicates the power he possesses (Claremont et al. 735–37).

Pérez's next creation relevant to the representation of race and ethnicity is also his most significant: Cyborg of the New Teen Titans. In contrast to White Tiger, Pérez was much more personally connected to the character of Cyborg/Victor Stone. Though Pérez was Puerto Rican and Stone black, both shared a common background. As Pérez himself notes, "since I grew up in the South Bronx, and [come] from a Puerto Rican background, I had a little more I could actually put into Cyborg's personality" (qtd. in Baker 45). Elsewhere, the artist elaborates on this connection: "Victor was an urban black man, and I was an urban Puerto Rican with the same type of background" (qtd. in Lawrence 52). However, locating Cyborg within an urban locale does not always appear benign. Pérez offers readers their first glimpse of Victor's New York City home—specifically at "44th street and Eleventh

Avenue"—in issue 3 of *The New Teen Titans*. On page 14, in the first panel—a vertical one stretching almost the entire height of the page—Cyborg sits on a fire escape above a trash-strewn alley surrounded by various brick-and-mortar buildings, some of them cracked and crumbling. The next panel shows similar cracks on the outside of Victor's apartment, cracks that also appear on its inside in panel 4; the same visual depiction reoccurs in issue 8, where the issue's narration underlines the nature of Stone's residence, describing it as "a dirty, filth-ridden reminder that riches and squalor exist side by side" (Wolfman et al. 1: 92, 218). The visual and other depictions of Cyborg's home both distinguish him from his fellow Titans—all of whom are comfortably middle class if not super wealthy, as in the case of Robin and Changeling—and connect him to a pattern surrounding black and other nonwhite superheroes in the 1970s and 1980s that links them to similarly depicted spaces (see Austin and Hamilton 163–65, 182).

Cyborg likewise plays into a kind of exoticism that results from his being among the other new additions Wolfman and Pérez added to the team. As Jonathan W. Gray explains, "Pérez designed each of the new additions to the team . . . to evoke diversity, and they are far more visually distinctive than their more venerable teammates. . . . Cyborg's visual distinctiveness helps establish this iteration of the Teen Titans as truly new and signals that the creators intend to tell a more progressive kind of superhero story" (126–27). There are pitfalls, though, to the idea of Cyborg and these other new characters as representing diversity. Cyborg being black, and the only one of the new characters identifiably raced, participates in a codification of race as "exotic," which is critiqued by bell hooks. As she writes, "ethnicity becomes spice, seasoning that can liven up the dull dish that is mainstream culture" (hooks 21). This is quite literally a purpose Cyborg's and the other new Titans' appearances are meant to serve precisely because of how they play in contrast to the other Titans' whiteness. To paraphrase both Gray and hooks, Cyborg is brought in along with the others to "liven up" the "dull dish" that is the Titan's predominant whiteness.

Then there's also the idea of how these characters signal Wolfman and Pérez's progressive intent. There is a troubling superficiality to that intent, particularly as two of the three new characters are exoticized instead by their status as a literal alien (Starfire) or mystic (Raven). Singer, for example, in talking about another DC mainstay, the Legion of Super-Heroes, highlights their colorblind but ultimately rather empty progressivism: "For nearly twenty years, the Legion's supposed racial diversity was mitigated—if not virtually negated—by the fact that, of all the races represented in the comic, only one group existed in real life: the white characters" ("Black Skins" 110–11). Representing diversity via only imaginary/alien races that are green-skinned, orange-skinned, or blue- or yellow-skinned necessarily limits the creators' progressive intent as they can only imagine diversity in fantastic and thus unreal forms. The orange-skinned Starfire is the clearest example of how Pérez's cocreation and design of these characters fall into a similar trap. Cyborg, particularly because his design visually signals diversity, thus carries the full burden of speaking to more real-world forms of difference but also then ends up as an almost overdetermined figure of such difference by being the only example.

Despite how Cyborg can be seen as ensnared within problematic representations and persistent stereotypes, aspects of Pérez's visualization of this new hero do work to combat these. A case in point would be Cyborg's very first appearance, which was in the third panel on page 3 of *The New Teen Titans* preview in *DC Comics Presents* no. 26. (It is also perhaps worth noting that Cyborg is the first of the three new Titans to appear and thus the first to offer a contrast to their whiteness). Here, as Pérez did with White Tiger, the artist conveys a power and confidence through how he positions Cyborg's body. He stands in the center of the panel, clearly the focus of it (and this despite Changeling perching as a green-skinned monkey on his left upper arm). His chest is broad, his left arm crooked as his left fist rests against his hip; his right arm is posed at a similar angle as his left but ends in an uplifted hand. The panel only depicts his upper legs, but they are muscular and firm, clearly indicating how he stands solidly and confidently before the more established Titans (Wolfman et al. 1: 14). Pérez poses Cyborg similarly throughout the series, creating a visual throughline indicating his strength, confidence, and resolve. In his first actual appearance in *The New Teen Titans* no. 1 (the preview story having been revealed as a Raven-induced vision), a series of four panels on page 11 depicts Victor removing his tracksuit to stand before Raven fully revealed. The final image clearly emphasizes Victor's strength: his muscular legs are again firmly planted, and he curls his arms, both ending in clenched fists (1: 37). In his expanded origin story in *Tales of the New Teen Titans* no. 1, Pérez, on page 23 of the issue, combines this posing with forced perspective, causing the reader (and Victor's opponents) to stare up at him, again standing resolutely before the moon and night sky. This same issue also includes a "Special Titans Pin-Up!" featuring Cyborg. Here, again, he stands heroically—legs straight and planted, arms slightly curled and spread, fists clenched— before a blueprint detailing his various cybernetic enhancements (1: 592, 676).

Besides emphasizing Cyborg/Victor Stone's heroic qualities of strength, confidence, and determination, Pérez imbues this new hero with a kinetic quality and energy via his art. It is this that the splash page to *Tales of the New Teen Titans* no. 1 emphasizes. Here, Pérez draws Cyborg leaping across the Grand Canyon and toward the reader (Wolfman et al. 1: 570). Cyborg leaping from or across the page is another common occurrence throughout the series linked to his kinetic nature. A particularly striking example occurs in *The New Teen Titans* no. 30 as Victor leaves the apartment of his friend Sarah Simms. A half-page panel at the top of page 13 depicts him leaping away, the New York City skyline lit up before a magenta sky in the background (figure 2.2). Here, Cyborg again moves with great thrust, his chin up, torso bent forward, arms spread to each side, and his left leg bent. His right leg, somewhat more extended than the other, actually breaks outside of the panel

Figure 2.2. Cyborg leaping away from the city and out of the panel from *The New Teen Titans*, vol. 1, no. 30, 1983 (Wolfman et al. 2: 285).

containing the rest of him, creating an almost 3D effect of Victor leaping not just over the city but also out of the very panel/page (2: 285). As Hatfield notes, bodies overlapping and thus breaking out of panel borders contribute to the dynamism within Kirby's art (24), and the same can be said of Pérez's work.

Pérez achieves similar kinetic effects when depicting Cyborg in battle. One such instance occurs over a series of three panels in *The New Teen Titans* preview. As the rest of the team battles futilely against an extradimensional protoplasmic blob, Cyborg leaps into action, thrusting his right arm into the creature in order to blast it with "a zillion decibels of white sound" (Wolfman et al. 1: 21). The last panel of this sequence is particularly kinetic: Cyborg leans forward, left leg bent in front of him, right leg extended behind, his torso and right arm thrust toward the creature as it explodes in pain. Another example is the two-page splash page for *The New Teen Titans* no. 39. Here, the Titans raid one of their enemy Brother Blood's secret facilities and confront his guards, who are disguised as American military personnel. Cyborg, positioned in the foreground of the telescoping image, leaps down from the top of the page, ready for battle: his fists are ready, raised above his head, and he kicks his right leg out toward a group of attackers. The telescoped nature of the page only adds to the thrusting motion with which Cyborg leaps as it funnels the action of the page toward him via its angular perspective (2: 564–65). In sum, even if other aspects of Cyborg's depiction in the series lean into stereotypes and problematic patterns, Pérez regularly depicts Cyborg heroically: powerful, determined, and with a kind of profound momentum to how he moves.

Another black hero Pérez helped create later in his career falls into similar patterns—for good and ill—as Cyborg. In the late 1990s, Pérez, with writer Kurt Busiek, helped introduce another African American hero, Triathlon, who debuted in issue 8 of their *Avengers* (1998) run. There, Triathlon aids the team against a group of armored operatives attacking Kennedy Airport and working for Power Man and X-Men foe Moses Magnum, eventually pursuing them on his own by stowing away on their hijacked aircraft. In the next issue, Triathlon alerts the Avengers to Magnum and his men's location and assists in defeating them. Over the course of this two-issue debut, readers learn both Triathlon's abilities and origin. Regarding the former, he tells the team that he's "three times as strong, fast and agile as an ordinary human" in issue 8 (Busiek and Pérez 1: 14). As for his origin, he explains to Hawkeye, in the next issue, that he is disgraced Olympian Delroy Garrett Jr., who was caught using steroids to compete in Olympic track competitions. Stripped of his medals and banned from competition, Delroy found his way to the Triune Understanding, a quasi-religious organization that, as he further details, "showed me a way to find peace, to let go of the anger I had towards myself—and in time—a way to unlock the power within me" (1: 10).[6] Triathlon's second appearance comes in *Avengers* no. 15 as the team pursues Lord Templar to the Triune headquarters. There, the team finds itself caught between Lord Templar and the brutish Pagan, but Triathlon prevents the team from interfering. At the issue's end, the Avengers find themselves at odds with the Triunes and their hero Triathlon, a conflict that will eventually culminate in Triathlon joining the team as of issue 27. Triathlon remained an Avenger through issue 54, the end of Busiek's Kang War storyline and long after Pérez's departure from the title, which occurred with issue 34.

Despite the close to twenty years since Cyborg's debut, Triathlon can be said to fall into many of the same problematic and stereotypical patterns that plague black and other nonwhite heroes, particularly as members of super teams. He has, from the start, a divisive and even antagonistic relationship with the other Avengers that trades in aspects of the "angry-black-man" stereotype. The cover of his first appearance symbolizes this: the then current Avengers roster stands in the background, posed in ways expressive of shock and consternation, as Triathlon, fore-grounded, pushes his way through and past them, saying "Step aside, heroes—Triathlon is coming through" (Busiek and Pérez 1: n.p.). In his first interactions with the team, Triathlon similarly expresses a kind of resentment. After freeing them from an energy prison in issue 8, he complains about their slowness in coming to his aid, as well as the fact that they get more press than he does (1: 13). And when he allies with the team again in issue 9, he replies to Hawkeye's apologies for his questions about the Triune Understanding with "You can't help being ignorant" (1: 11).

Surrounding Triathlon is also a suspicion and mystery that likewise sets him off from the Avengers. This distance if not exclusion is another pattern black and other nonwhite heroes have replicated again and again within supposedly multicultural super teams (Austin and Hamilton 179). Because of this suspicion, Triathlon is always a little bit "off" in relation to the other heroes in the title. The first real sense of this suspicion comes in issue 9 when Triathlon breaks into the Avengers' internal communications frequency to alert them to Magnum's location, an action both Captain America and Iron Man question, particularly as they only met Triathlon the day before and never gave him access to this waveband (Busiek and Pérez 1: 7). Triathlon is again depicted at odds with the Avengers when he returns in issue 15. The Avengers, having tracked Lord Templar's energy signature to the Triune Compound, are rebuffed by the new hero in their attempts to continue their pursuit, Triathlon asking Cap directly, "Just what are you accusing the Triune Understanding of, anyway?" (1: 11). The battle that ensues between the Avengers, Pagan, and Lord Templar further antagonizes relations between the heroes as Triathlon puts himself between the Avengers and the two opponents, telling them that he will stop anyone that tries to intervene in their battle (1: 17). At the end of the issue, as the Triune Understanding's leader, Jonathan Tremont, disparages the Avengers during a press conference, Triathlon stands silent but with a seemingly smug smile on his face; the next page's revelation that Tremont and Lord Templar (and, as will later be revealed, Pagan) are physically linked only adds to the suspicion and doubt these brief appearances have already layered onto Triathlon (1: 20–21).

When Triathlon officially joins the Avengers with issue 27, he not only continues the above patterns but falls into another one, that of the token member. In doing so, he implicitly recalls an earlier *Avengers* plot from the late 1970s that saw the Falcon forced onto the team by the US government; here, history repeats itself as the Avengers' current government liaison, Duane Turner, convinces the Avengers they must add Triathlon to their ranks. The series even makes explicit the connection between the two stories, as Pérez depicts Triathlon looking at a photo from Falcon's short-lived stint with the team (Busiek and Pérez 2: 16). His Avengers status, however, does little to curb the problematic tendencies already exhibited in his depiction. He joins, telling the Avengers he's lost some of the respect he had for them and that he joined to prove them wrong about the Triunes as well, and adds, "and then I'm going to rub your noses in it!" (2: 19). Such antagonism would continue throughout Triathlon's time with the team. As the Avengers, in issue 28, demolish a series of buildings as a promotional stunt, Triathlon not only chafes at the Wasp's orders but, in response to her concerns about his safety, replies, "Yeah, yeah, so, we about done here—or do you have more darkie labor for me?" (2: 6). He makes similarly racially charged comments as he collects water for the team (2: 21–22).

This situation then feeds into another common pattern involving such "token" heroes: the onus being put on them to resolve the conflict they didn't necessarily create. Such a pattern regularly appeared in comics of the 1970s and 1980s, particularly those espousing an ideal of "brotherhood" between nonwhites (most often blacks) and whites (Austin and Hamilton 114). And it again manifests in *Avengers* with Triathlon. In issue 29, Avengers member Warbird (Carol Danvers, nowadays Captain Marvel) lectures Triathlon about his fractious nature within the team, particularly taking him to task for the various racially charged comments he makes about his position and making it his responsibility to change (Busiek and Pérez 2: 14–15). Here, Danver's lecture echoes how, in previous decades, the obstacle to such brotherhood was most often pinned as the black individual's anger and resentment, something time and time again black people are depicted as having to overcome first before any kind of brotherhood can exist. This same pattern reoccurs at the end of issue 30 when Iron Man tries once again to mend things with Triathlon. Here, the response is different: whereas he previously slapped the armored Avenger's hand away, Triathlon accepts it (2: 22). Thus, in terms of how Triathlon is depicted within the narrative of *Avengers*, he falls into a variety of pernicious stereotypes and other patterns.

But though Triathlon, like Cyborg, replicates these patterns, Pérez's realization of this new hero works, also like Cyborg's, in contrast to them. Visually and physically, Triathlon is dynamic. The design of Triathlon's costume fully embraces the outré aspects of superhero fashion. Whereas White Tiger simply appears in white and Cyborg's costume blends seamlessly into his cybernetics, Triathlon's design mirrors the bright, multicolored outfits of other Pérez-designed heroes. His original suit is tricolored, with green and red running from his arms and sides, while black runs down the center of his torso and legs. He also sports a white chevron with gold trim across his shoulders and down to the center of his chest. In terms of a mask, Triathlon wears a black facemask, open at the top and around his nose and mouth, with a pair of green goggles over his eyes, as well as a pair of black gloves. And as a superhero with abilities based in his athleticism, Triathlon possesses an even greater sense of kinetic energy and movement than Cyborg. His first on-panel appearance in issue 8 is a half-page panel of the hero running toward the reader after freeing the assembled Avengers from an energy cage (figure 2.3). Pink and green speed lines matching the external colors of his uniform sweep around the page, indicating both Triathlon's speed and range. As well, given how Pérez overlaps one of the upper panels with Triathlon's right hand, he appears to almost be running off the page, not unlike the earlier-discussed panel from *The New Teen Titans* featuring a leaping Cyborg (Busiek and Pérez 1: 13).

Pérez again emphasizes Triathlon's athletic gifts when he returns in issue 15. Pérez also redesigns his costume, thus sharing with this character the Wasp's predilection for such variation. His torso design is now a series of chevrons—black around his neck and down his chest, green from his arms and shoulders down to his mid chest, and red from his mid torso to his waist—with a gold triangle in the center. His lower body is now mostly black with a green stripe running down the sides of his legs to his foot, with red on the interior forming a boot. The opening sequence of this issue portrays Triathlon performing a series of athletic feats. On the splash page, he leaps directly at the reader and, in a two-page sequence, leaps diagonally down from the upper left through a horizontal series of rings before landing, feet down and arms up in triumph, in the bottom right corner of the second page (Busiek

Figure 2.3. Triathlon's first appearance from *The Avengers*, vol. 3, no. 8, 1998 (Busiek and Pérez 1: n.p.).

and Pérez 1: 2–3). A later panel in the same issue again presents Triathlon transcending the confines of a panel. As he runs to confront the brutish Pagan, Triathlon's left foot extends beyond the borders, putting him not only in front of the background but escaping from the panel if not the entirety of the page (1: 12).

And while aspects of Triathlon's characterization play into established and problematic patterns, at least some of how Pérez represents the new hero among the team plays against other such

patterns. The ways in which he plays on the Falcon's brief original tenure with the team speak to this. As Allan W. Austin and
Patrick L. Hamilton point out, Falcon was largely marginalized
within the team: during half his tenure with the team, he didn't
participate in their battles and, when he did, was often depicted
behind his fellow Avengers (180–81). In contrast, there's the image
of the Avengers at the end of issue 27, announcing the new team.
Triathlon stands dead center, between founding Avengers Wasp
and Iron Man (Busiek and Pérez 2: 21). The next issue, he plays as
much a role as any other member in the new team's first action,
running through the interior of the building they combine to
demolish, knocking out the central support pillars (2: 5). The cover
to issue 29 similarly spotlights Triathlon. Pérez draws the team in
a circular pattern that again puts Triathlon toward the front as
his body clearly overlaps those of She-Hulk, Giant-Man, and the
Scarlet Witch (2: n.p.). The ways in which Triathlon differs from
Falcon are significant because they both join the Avengers under
a cloud of unwelcome and/or suspicion. In the case of Falcon, this
cloud is reflected in how various artists depicted his place on the
team, while Pérez counters that with Triathlon by consistently
depicting him as a full-fledged member despite the circumstances
under which he joined.

Such counterbalancing of problematic narratives and representations concerning race thus is a throughline of Pérez's depictions
and cocreation of these various racialized heroes. Even if characters
like the Sons of the Tiger, White Tiger, Cyborg, and Triathlon
replicate persistent and problematic narratives concerning race
within their various narratives, Pérez routinely strives to coun-
terbalance these pernicious patterns in his artwork. He thus finds
visual ways of conveying strength, confidence, and, perhaps most
importantly, equality even when those grate against other aspects
of their depiction.

Titans Together:
Cyborg, Jericho, and Narratives of Disability

In *Death, Disability, and the Superhero: The Silver Age and Beyond*, José Alaniz describes the superhero, from its very beginning, as a form of representation that denies disabled bodies and privileges healthy ones. In fact, "by the very logic of the narrative," superheroes actively erase "normal, mortal flesh in favor of a quasi-fascist physical ideal" (Alaniz 6). Implicit within Alaniz's description is how that physical ideal is codified in comic book art; the physical perfection that the logic of the superhero genre requires is made manifest in superheroes'—male and female—manifestation on the comic book page. Thus, as was the case above when it comes to race, the verbal and visual aspects of comics often conspire within superhero narratives to promulgate this erasure (as well as other problematic representations) of disability. And as was also the case above, Pérez can, at times, be seen in his artwork as diverging from and even challenging the disservice comics have generally done to differently abled persons and bodies. Most prominent in these efforts are two of Pérez's cocreations for *The New Teen Titans*: the aforementioned Cyborg/Victor Stone and Jericho/Joseph Wilson.

It is not the case that everything Pérez did in terms of representing disability deviated from comics' norms. Pérez's revamp of Barbara Minerva/Cheetah in *Wonder Woman*, for instance, trades in many existing and problematic tropes related to disability. Her introduction on pages 21 and 22 to close issue 7 depicts her as largely bedridden and carrying a visual signal of disability, a cane (Pérez et al., *Wonder Woman* 181–82). She uses the cane at various points throughout her cameos in issue 8 and then in issue 9, where she eventually becomes the Cheetah and confronts Wonder Woman before disappearing for the remainder of Pérez's run as writer and artist. Besides the cane, there is no explicit mention of Minerva's disability. On page 6 of issue 8, her dialogue does reference "body aches" and then, on pages 6 and 7 of issue 9, she falls to the ground after suffering the effects of Diana's lasso of truth, clinging to a banister while lying on the floor; Chuma, a West African pygmy that serves Minerva, then approaches her from behind with her cane (189, 212–13). In this, Minerva's markers of disability function as what David T. Mitchell and Sharon L. Snyder define as a "narrative prosthesis," in which disability appears as a marker of a character, something that distinguishes them and generates the/their story but then is largely forgotten once that difference is established (qtd. in Alaniz and Smith 6, see also 8). Furthermore, the use of disability here hearkens back to the Golden Age of comics when, as José Alaniz and Scott T. Smith point out: "the disabled figure almost never steps out from under the penumbra of perfidy. Disability as a facet of human corporeal/cognitive existence entered the genre as a blatant and simplistic marker of evil" (2). Pérez's Minerva follows in a long line of disabled/disfigured comic book villains, her impairment perhaps not as monstrously depicted as others but still, along with her imperious and devious character, functioning almost ubiquitously as a facet of her evil.

When it comes to Cyborg's representation of disability, scholars have been divided, particularly regarding his relationship to the "supercrip." There are those that see his character as the very definition of the "supercrip," the disabled character whose overcoming of their disability is celebrated and inspiring. Lauren O'Connor, for example, sees Cyborg as a repetition and reification of this figure, one who thus underlines "the can-do spirit of American bootstrap mythology" in how he overcomes his disability (113). Jonathan W. Gray similarly dubs Cyborg "a 'supercrip' par excellence" for how his very definition as a superhero is based in learning how to use the technological implants that make him not only more than his disability but, ultimately, more than human (125–26). At the same time, there are scholars who appear more rehabilitative in their assessments of Cyborg. Marit Hanson, in discussing DC's Barbara Gordon/Batgirl/Oracle, lumps Cyborg along with other disabled heroes as part of a norm in comics where such cybernetic enhancements render the subject more than human (95, 107).

Alaniz likewise appears to see value in Cyborg's representation. In particular and drawing largely from his origin story in *Tales of the New Teen Titans* no. 1, Alaniz credits Cyborg's depiction as putting "a new emphasis on the psychological labor of 'overcoming' massive injury, as well as a graphic depiction of trauma, recovery, and adjustment to new physical realities" (49). Thus, though all see Cyborg as, in one way or another, relating to the "supercrip" stereotype, they vary in the degree of nuance they interpret as present within his character.

Disability as a narrative prosthesis is another danger Cyborg's representation risks. The supercrip's bootstrap narrative pulls attention away from the lived reality of disabled persons that O'Connor identifies as a threat: "These characters serve as allegorical 'outsiders,' stand-ins for various marginalized groups but rarely for actual disabled people—their disabilities are . . . metaphoric devices" that substitute for the lived reality of disability (119–20). In the case of narrative prosthesis, disability similarly remains only a device that is at best metaphorical or allegorical in its treatment of disability. In other words, even if Cyborg is a representation of disability, his representation doesn't really reflect or say anything about the lived reality of being disabled. Like so many other disabled heroes, Cyborg's nature as a superhero—in this case, his cybernetic enhancements—more than compensate for his status as a quadriplegic so that, in a way, he both is and is not disabled. Even when his cybernetic arms and legs are destroyed in the course of various adventures with his fellow Titans, it is a very short time before he or someone else is able to make the necessary repairs. A particularly telling example occurs in *The New Teen Titans* nos. 23 and 24, when the team first confronts Starfire's villainous sister Blackfire. At the end of the first issue, Blackfire's drones sever both of Cyborg's legs at the knee. The splash page of the next issue depicts the still legless Cyborg being carried by Wonder Girl and Kid Flash; however, by the third page of this same issue, Cyborg's legs are reattached, and his disability is once again made largely invisible (Wolfman et al. 2: 85, 89, 92).

To his credit, Pérez can be said to take steps toward redressing these prosthetic uses of disability inherent in Cyborg's character. These above assessments largely look at Cyborg and disability through the lens of his superhero identity; however, how the character represents disability also takes place outside of his identity as Cyborg and Teen Titan and thus within the portrayal of his civilian identity as Victor Stone. It is through depicting Stone as a civilian that Pérez contributes to the discourse surrounding disability. Though Pérez is often thought of as drawing large action sequences and event comics, he pays just as much, if not more, attention to the civilian/personal lives of his characters. This was especially true during his time on *The New Teen Titans*. As he explains, it was this emphasis on the lives of the characters that was another factor in developing his artistic style: "It wasn't until the characters started having real personal lives, which I treasured and loved to illustrate, that I flourished" (Pérez and Biggers 102). This attention to the personal lives of his characters is yet another aspect of Pérez's knack for storyworld building as they too speak to a larger world and narrative around but separate from the superheroic action. When it comes to Cyborg, Pérez's personal touch also proffers somewhat of a corrective to the ways in which his representation of disability often proves problematic.

This alternative representation comes most fully in the "day-in-the-life" segments of *The New Teen Titans* issue 8. The plot of this issue focuses on the personal lives of the Titans, jumping back and forth between the various members as they spend a day largely without traditional superhero conflicts. The bulk of Cyborg's narrative in this issue occurs on pages 12–15 and features two scenes. The first has Victor showing up at the apartment of his former girlfriend Marcy, whom he has not seen since the accident that led to his cybernetic implants. Their reunion does not go well. Marcy is horrified by Victor's appearance and reveals that she dropped all contact with him at the insistence of her parents. After Victor leaves Marcy's home, he has a second encounter, this one in a park when a baseball bounces off his head. This leads to him meeting Sarah Simms and her students, all of whom have prosthetic limbs. The sequence ends with Stone taking off his coat and hat and leading the students toward the baseball diamond to continue their game (Wolfman et al. 1: 220–23). Wolfman credits Pérez with the creation of this sequence. In his introduction to the omnibus collection containing this issue, Wolfman explains how he and Pérez had discussed the story for this issue but that there was no specific plot written. As a result, he details, "George not only came up with the sequence but told it magnificently" (1: 9). Similarly, Wolfman in Lawrence's *George Pérez: Storyteller* describes this part of the narrative as "absolutely all George" (qtd. on 49).

And at least visually, the park sequence that starts at the bottom of page 13 and runs through the top two-thirds of page 15 offers some small correction of the series' representation of disability to this point. The scene juxtaposes Victor Stone/Cyborg's more fantastical and thus less realistic visualization of prosthetic compensation with those of the children. In this, the sequence at least suggests the presence of disabilities more akin to those in lived experience. The dialogue, at least at one point, appears to underline this point. As Victor hands an errant baseball to the first young child he meets, his metal hand is exposed. Far from the fear Stone expects, the boy reacts with fascination. He says, in the first panel depicting his reaction, about Victor's hand: "Wow, it's real neat. I wish they gave me one like that." This is followed, in the second, by "I mean, all they gave me was this reg'lar one." When the other students and their teacher Sarah Simms arrive, the boy reiterates this contrast, telling her and his fellow students: "He's just like us. He's got a pros . . . a new hand, too. Only his is real shiny, an' real neat" (Wolfman et al. 1: 222). Here, Wolfman's dialogue underlines what Pérez's artwork also emphasizes: the fact that Victor Stone/ Cyborg is not a realistic representation of disability. His cybernetic enhancements are more "shiny" and "neat" than those the children possess, descriptions that play upon and thus emphasize Stone/Cyborg's fantastical nature when it comes to representing disability. In this, the sequence Pérez creates in this issue takes a stab—intentional or otherwise—at addressing how Cyborg's disability otherwise falls into the tradition of a narrative prosthetic. It at least introduces into the comic book storyworld of *The New Teen Titans* more realistic forms of prosthetic limbs and thus more realistically depicted forms of disability. Even if the dialogue slips backward later in this sequence—Simms talking about how the students are there to "relearn things . . . to show them they can lead a full life again," thus "almost forgetting their problems," all of which echoes the common bootstrap/overcoming narrative—the visual sequence Pérez created and upon which the dialogue was later imposed at least gestures toward a representation of disability less based in these problematic patterns (1: 223).

Pérez's art takes advantage of the further interactions between Cyborg and Sarah Simms's students to continue contrasting their representations of disability. One of these interactions comes the very next issue. This sequence occurs at Simms's school, where both Cyborg and Raven are visitors (figure 2.4). In the first panel on page 9, Cyborg kneels down to help one of the students with his jacket while Raven sits to the right behind him next to another student. In the center of the panel, and thus to the left of Cyborg, stand Simms and two other students, one wearing a sling. Visually, Cyborg strikingly contrasts the rest of these surroundings. He crouches but his cybernetics are fully on display and even gleaming. The rest of the characters—Simms, the students, and even Raven—appear much more normally dressed (Wolfman et al. 1: 243). Again, the visuals reinforce Victor/Cyborg's extraordinary and fantastical nature, here by foregrounding it against much more ordinary-appearing surroundings and individuals. An exchange between Raven and the student wearing a sling again underlines the ways in which superhero representations of disability contrast lived experience of the same. The student asks Raven, who has the ability to heal others by taking their pain into herself, if she can provide her with a new hand, a request Raven states is beyond her ability. An ensuing conversation between her and Cyborg can be read as another underlining of how superhero solutions to

Figure 2.4. Cyborg and Raven visit Sarah Simms's school from *The New Teen Titans*, vol. 1, no. 9, 1981 (Wolfman et al. 1: 243).

disability ring hollow in contrast to reality. He explains how the students had been asking for Raven to come see them for some time in expectation of the kind of miracle superheroes often provide (1: 243). Thus, Raven can be seen not only as providing such a lesson to Simms's students but also as emphasizing the paucity inherent within representations of disability, such as Cyborg's, that gloss over realities of living with disabilities.

From this point, however, the opportunities for this contrast to be furthered are limited. Two plot contrivances keep Simms and her school, and thus their relationship with and to Cyborg, absent from the series. First, in issue 10, Simms is kidnapped by Titans' enemy Deathstroke the Terminator and used as leverage to trap the team. Following their rescue of Simms and subversion of Deathstroke's plans, Cyborg avoids contact with Simms, feeling guilty that she found herself endangered because of him. But even once Cyborg and Simms reconcile, events continue to keep them apart, as, in issue 30, Cyborg encounters a man in her apartment claiming to be her fiancé, and it is not until issue 35 of the first volume of the series before this misunderstanding is similarly resolved. This leads to the final appearance of Simms's students on pages 6 and 7 in issue 42 and thus the final opportunity for their contrast with Stone to be continued during Pérez's first run on the title. Here, though, their interaction is mainly played for laughs as Stone, unable to ice skate, finds himself falling flat on his back on the ice, surrounded by the amused Simms as well as her students, one of whom calls Stone "out" like an umpire on a baseball field. Pérez does provide one panel that might be said to continue the meaningful contrast between Stone and the disabled students: in it, he stands uneasily, supporting himself on the ice by grasping at the various students, who appear untroubled by the ice (Wolfman et al. 2: 16–17).

If Victor Stone/Cyborg is a perhaps, at best, mixed representation of disability, it would be Pérez's cocreation of another Titan with a disability that would prove more successful. This character is Joseph/Joe Wilson, a.k.a Jericho, later revealed to be the youngest son of Deathstroke. Kidnapped as a child by an international terrorist known as the Jackal to use as leverage against his father, Joseph had his vocal cords severed, rendering him mute, during Deathstroke's effort to rescue him. Alaniz lists Jericho among other "sensibility-challenging, button-pushing" characters from the 1980s (among which he also includes Cyborg) and likewise christens him, after the silent Inhuman Black Bolt, "the most prominent mute character in the genre, often shown using sign language" (157). In fact, Wolfman and Pérez had an agreement not to use thought bubbles or similar devices to get around Joseph's muteness. This can be seen as another step toward greater representation of the lived reality of disability—in this case, muteness—as it avoids the kind of shortcuts that often render other representations problematic. Unlike, say, with Cyborg's cybernetic limbs that essentially and unrealistically compensate for his loss of arms and legs or Daredevil's radar sense that allows him to largely not function as a blind man, Wolfman and Pérez made representing Jericho's disability more realistically a priority of their depiction.

The result was also a character and portrayal that relied even more heavily on Pérez as an artist. In many ways, Jericho/Joseph Wilson is even more of a Pérez creation than the other Titans. As Wolfman describes, "If Raven was mine, Jericho was George's baby" (Wolfman et al. 3: 8). Pérez provides further details of his contribution to Jericho's creation. As Pérez explains in his introduction to the third *New Teen Titans* omnibus volume, Wolfman came up with the character's name and connection to Deathstroke, but the rest of what would come to define this character proved difficult for his creators to determine. That is until a moment of inspiration hit Pérez, and he, "overnight," came up with "the concept, personality, and design for Joseph William Wilson" (3: 10). Echoing Wolfman, Pérez describes Jericho as "more of an artist's character than a writer's character"; as well, he presented challenges to Pérez as an artist that he formerly would not have felt up to: "I was forced to convey Jericho's personality through body language and facial expressions. Such subtle nuances would have been unthinkable for me when I first started the series in 1980" (3: 10). Ironically, Pérez left *The New Teen Titans* soon after Jericho's debut. Only the back of Wilson's head appears in one panel at the end of issue 42, and he appears on a mere handful of pages in issue 43 before debuting fully in issue 44, which provides his origin. After that, Pérez only drew issues 45–47 fully and contributed only six and seven pages to no. 48 and no. 49 before the oversized issue 50 ended his run on the first volume of *The New Teen Titans*. Pérez then moved over to the art duties on the second volume of the series but left *Titans* completely after that series' fifth issue. In all, then, Pérez's initial depiction of Jericho amounts to a little over twelve issues or roughly one year of the series. However, even this relatively brief stint reveals ways in which Pérez's efforts contributed to a more positive depiction of his disability.

As previously mentioned, an important aspect of Pérez and Wolfman's approach to Jericho is not relying on thought balloons as a means by which to circumvent his mute status. This is not, however, the only way the creators avoid reducing Wilson's muteness to the status of another narrative prosthetic. Jericho's powers provide another potential way to circumvent his disability. Jericho has the ability to enter and thus control another person's body when he makes direct eye contact with them. Jericho also thus gains the ability to speak through any body he inhabits. One can easily see how this aspect of Jericho's power could subvert his disability: he could easily take over another's body and thus have restored, in a sense, his voice. In this, Jericho could potentially mirror Marvel's Daredevil as the kind of disabled character whose disability (in Daredevil's case, blindness) is overcome via the nature of other superhuman gifts. To their credit, Wolfman and Pérez generally avoid this trap. When, in *The New Teen Titans Annual* no. 3, the conclusion to the famed Judas Contract storyline, Jericho takes over the body of a miscellaneous member of H.I.V.E., the criminal organization that plagued the Titans and set Deathstroke on their trail since issue 2, he further explains the nature of his power. Most relevantly, he explains to Nightwing on page 14 of the issue that when he takes over another person who has been rendered unconscious, he can talk "but in their voice, with their words" (Wolfman et al. 3: 100). Thus, even though Jericho does speak, he doesn't speak as he himself would; similar to the avoidance of thought balloons, Wolfman and Pérez likewise avoid having Jericho take possession of another person—be it a villain or ally—in order to express himself in a way he otherwise cannot.

Pérez's artwork is another means by which Jericho's expression is achieved without resorting to the kinds of shortcuts plaguing other disabled characters. One such example comes during a scene on pages 14–15 in *Tales of the Teen Titans* no. 45.[7] Here, Jericho picks up Raven from Manhattan College, where she is a student, though Raven suddenly disappears from the car when summoned to Titans Tower. Following her departure, there is a four-panel sequence at the bottom of the page that focuses on Wilson: in the first panel, he sees the books Raven left behind when she teleported, then in the second, he holds up one of them, showing it to be a book on learning sign language, followed by a close up

THERE IS *FEAR* IN WILSON'S WIDE GREEN EYES AS HIS THROAT MAKES WILD, RASPING SOUNDS THAT FORM NO WORDS...

...AND HIS FINGERS TWIST AND DANCE, DESPERATELY SEARCHING FOR CONCEPTS NO *SIGN LANGUAGE* WAS DESIGNED TO CONVEY.

JOEY, SLOW DOWN! DAMN! HE'S SIGNING TOO FAST FOR ME TO FOLLOW.

Figure 2.5. Jericho after exiting Raven's soul from *The New Teen Titans*, vol. 2, no. 1, 1984 (Wolfman et al. 1: 492).

on his face in the third before shifting to a final exterior shot of the car as it races toward Titans Tower as well (Wolfman et al. 3: 142). What's interesting about this sequence is how Pérez's art is sufficient to convey the significance of this moment. Though Wolfman adds narrative captions explaining the effect—specifically illustrating the bond already starting to exist between Jericho and Raven and how it counters Raven's supposedly unemotional nature—the images themselves by and large convey these themes. Pérez is able to thus visually convey the emotional thrust of this moment in a way that renders the gilding by Wolfman's captions unnecessary. Other moments do much the same, such as pages 23 and 24 that end issue 48. Here, Jericho approaches the doorway to Raven's room holding a wrapped gift for Donna Troy and her soon-to-be husband, Terry Long. He pauses, and the look on his face in the third panel very much evokes the sense of worry and concern he again feels toward Raven. The center panel on the next page, paralleling Jericho to Raven as both hold their hands up to the door between them, is similarly evocative particularly of the former's clear care for the latter (3: 223–24). Crucially, Jericho remains silent throughout this sequence and, but for the narrative captions around the earlier closeup of his face, completely reliant on Pérez's visuals for how he expresses himself. Similar moments occur in the first issue of the second volume of *The New Teen Titans*. Twice in this issue, Jericho enters Raven's soul, which her demonic father, Trigon, has more and more control of, and he comes out absolutely terrified. In panels on page 7 (figure 2.5) and 22, Pérez—now, in many ways, at the top of his game—captures Jericho's abject fear, his eyes wide and mouth slack with terror (3: 492, 507).

Even if the plot falls prey to the limits of the discourses around disability and race, Pérez does, at times, find ways and/or make efforts to positively contribute to comics' representations of racial and bodily differences. This thus sets the stage for what is perhaps his most profound contribution to the history of representation in comics: his guidance of the post–*Crisis on Infinite Earths* relaunch of DC mainstay Wonder Woman through which Pérez consciously sought to advance the representation of gender and women in particular in similar but also more significant ways.

CHAPTER THREE

From Wonder(s) to Sirens

Representing Gender

With a forty-plus-year career in comics, Pérez had ample time to contribute to the visual representation of gender, particularly that of women. Pérez's run on DC's *Wonder Woman* is often perceived as the peak of this effort. Carolyn Cocca includes a brief discussion of Pérez's *Wonder Woman* in her discussion of 1980s and 1990s *Wonder Woman* comics, touting him as a "self-described feminist" and describing his Wonder Woman as combining feminine and masculine traits (37). Enrique García likewise focuses on Pérez's reboot, juxtaposing it with the work of Jaime Hernandez in challenging not only gendered but also racial, ethnic, and nationalist biases within comics (163). Pérez's time on *Wonder Woman* is certainly an apex not only within his representation of gender but also within his career; however, Pérez's self-conscious efforts to remedy the vexed history of comics' representation of gender are not unique to this run. They predate it in how Pérez became more and more self-conscious about distinguishing male and female bodies up through his time on *The New Teen Titans*. And it continues, post–*Wonder Woman*, through any number of projects, including his final published work, the six-issue Boom! Studios series *George Pérez's Sirens*, which is just as concerned with gender and gendered depictions of superheroines as anything else in his oeuvre.

Bodies in Motion:
Pérez and Distinguishing Gendered Forms

Just as Pérez evolved his style in general, his representation of both male and female figures is an area in which his art similarly developed. Throughout a lot of his early career in comics (and thus at Marvel), Pérez drew similar body types for each of his male and female characters, as an image from *Avengers* no. 149 aptly demonstrates (figure 3.1). Here, the bulk of the current team has been captured by the Roxxon Corporation and bound to an "electroincinerogram." Their lined-up forms showcase the similarity with which Pérez drew male and female bodies. In both cases, there is a roundedness to their physique but in different ways. With the men—from left to right, the Beast, Vision, Captain America, and Iron Man—this roundedness is most prominent in their shoulders, biceps, and chest regardless of whether they are mutant,

Figure 3.1. The Avengers held captive by Roxxon from *The Avengers*, vol. 1, no. 149, 1976 (Englehart et al. 465).

synthezoid, supersoldier, or clad in sophisticated armor. The legs of the men are likewise all of a type: muscular cylindrical thighs and calves that are another hallmark of the Pérez male physique. With female superheroes, as demonstrated in this same image by Hellcat and the Scarlet Witch, this roundedness is most obvious in their breasts, which are perfectly spherical. One also sees it in their hips particularly as a result of how their waist narrows just above them and tapered, cylindrical, and nonmuscular legs descend from them (Englehart et al. 465).

Pérez does acknowledge these limitations in his early work. For example, he talks about how he recognized this as a deficit in his art when working on the 1977 *Logan's Run* adaptation. In order to become a better artist, Pérez notes retrospectively how, among other things, his younger self would "have to spend a little more time understanding the anatomy" and "find a way of making women look different from each other, men look different from each other, as opposed to just hairstyle" (qtd. in Baker 34–35). Some of this again resulted from the particular conditions Pérez worked at while at Marvel. For one, he was, at least early on, working on not only team books like *Avengers*, *Fantastic Four*, and *Inhumans* with large casts but also some if not all of these and other titles at the same time. Such demands cannot help but to have encouraged a similarity of representation in order to meet deadlines. Additionally, there was again the pressure imposed by the Marvel "house style," something Pérez often chafed against. As he describes, in those early days at Marvel, what would become the recognizable George Pérez style "hadn't been developed as distinctively," and "I was working in some elements of a house style rather than drawing for myself" (Pérez and Biggers 36). So, the sameness that limited Pérez's representation of male and female bodies was in part a product of his inexperience as an artist but also various conditions under which he worked at the time.

As with so many things in Pérez's work and life, that all changed with his move from Marvel to DC. The freedom he enjoyed as a creator at his new company—freedom from doing multiple titles, from a house style, etc.—allowed him to develop in many ways as an artist. Those ways include how he visualized and depicted gendered bodies. We can see this development occurring on the very pages of *The New Teen Titans*. At the start of the series, that sameness of representation is still very much present. The cover of *The New Teen Titans* no. 1 manifests this tendency in Pérez's work. In a shot of the teen heroes moving toward the reader, Pérez aligns them by gender: the four male characters—from left to right, Kid Flash, Robin, Changeling, and Cyborg—run on the ground while the three women in the series—Starfire, Raven, and Wonder Girl—fly above them. Their positioning allows for the similarities in body type within each gender to stand out. Though Cyborg appears larger in both his upper and lower body, Kid Flash and Robin have very much the same physique. The rounded shoulders and biceps are again present here, as are the muscled legs. Similarly, the three women all possess the spherical breasts, narrowed waist, and rounded hips that featured in Pérez's women at this point (Wolfman et al. 1: 26). These similarities and even some incongruities continue in the pages Pérez drew behind this cover. One particularly incongruous image occurs at the bottom of page 9 of the Titans' introduction. The reunited Robin, Kid Flash, Changeling, and Wonder Girl again race toward the reader in the final panel. However, Kid Flash is a stack of muscle. His arms, chest, and particularly his legs are profoundly muscular and not what one might expect of a typical runner's body, whether or not they possess superspeed. In the horizontal panel two panels above this one, Kid Flash and Changeling possess similarly muscular and sized chests and arms despite the latter being significantly younger than the former (1: 35). The title's second issue likewise showcases the continued similarity in how Pérez drew his female characters. Several panels on pages 4 and 5 of this issue depict Starfire, Wonder Girl, and the civilian Carol, the ex-girlfriend of Grant Wilson, whose apartment the wounded Starfire crashed into and where she now convalesces. All three are again quite similar, as can be seen in panels 4 and 6 on page 4 and the second panel on page 5, where the trio are lined up next to each other (1: 56, 57).

Eventually, though, Pérez introduced variations in the physical appearance of the characters in *The New Teen Titans*, particularly the female heroes. As the characters began to develop and differ in terms of their personality, so too did Pérez start to differentiate their bodies. As Wolfman explains, "George, when he got on the Titans, not only saw the characters as individuals; he realized . . . that if Raven was one type of character, she needed to have a physical type that reflected her personality" (qtd. in Lawrence 53). Pérez similarly describes his efforts in this regard: "I was trying to draw them as real teens and trying to develop different body languages, body styles, body types" (qtd. on 54). The evidence of Pérez's effort was not long in coming. A splash page in issue 19, for instance, showcases some ways the artist began to distinguish characters like Starfire and Wonder Girl (figure 3.2). As Wonder Girl flies beside and behind Starfire, their respective breast size is immediately distinct as Starfire's bust appears significantly larger. Two inset panels showing a close-up of each woman's face make clear further differences. Wonder Girl has a slightly more pointed chin in contrast to Starfire's slightly more rounded one, and Starfire's face appears slightly wider than her teammate's (Wolfman et al. 1: 524).

But the most profound changes in appearance among the Titans' female cast occurred in Raven. At the start of the series, she has as rounded, curved, and buxom a figure as the other female characters. Her face likewise has similarly rounded and soft features, as evidenced in issue 4, for example, when, on pages 6 and 9, she removes her hood (Wolfman et al. 1: 110, 113). Soon, though, Pérez developed an even more distinctive look for Raven. This change is noticeable in issue 16, where, on page 3, she is shown in profile in panel 6 with decidedly sharper features and an even more pronounced eyebrow. In issue 18, she appears again without her hood and with a much more pronounced forehead as well as a generally stern expression, as conveyed by her sharp nose and somewhat

Figure 3.2. Starfire and Wonder Girl in flight from *The New Teen Titans*, vol. 1, no. 19, 1982 (Wolfman et al. 1: 524).

pursed lips (1: 438, 500). By issue 28, her look had evolved further. A sequence of panels on page 14 of the issue clearly demonstrates how her breasts have become flatter; a close-up on her face in the next row of panels also makes clear how her face and head have much more elongated and narrow looks to them (2: 238). These shifts in Raven's appearance eventually culminated in the plotline that would kick off the second volume of the title. As Wolfman sums it up: "George and I were looking at the evolution of his work on Raven, who began as a somewhat round-faced heroine with standard comic book good looks. We noticed that she now had a long, thin face. Her hair receded into a strong widow's peak. Her eyes had changed" (3: 9). On page 14 of the first issue of this second volume, Cyborg reviews various photos of the troubled Raven, identified as from issue 4 and issue 28 respectively along with a more recent one, that make clear her physical evolution (3: 499). Though, within the narrative, her physical transformation is indicative of the growing presence and power of her demonic father, Trigon, this is a plot that was derived from Pérez's development as an artist. As Wolfman goes on to note, this was a result of how Pérez increasingly treated each Titan as a "real individual" (3: 9). It is also testament to the ways in which Pérez worked to achieve a more nuanced representation of gender, particularly when it came to his female characters.

Resisting Comics' Gendered History:
Pérez's *Wonder Woman*

What Pérez began to achieve in relation to gender in *The New Teen Titans* set the stage for what would become his most signature work: the post–*Crisis on Infinite Earths* reboot of DC's *Wonder Woman*. Pérez came on to the *Wonder Woman* title at the nadir for the character. As a result of how *Crisis on Infinite Earths* had rebooted the DC comic book universe, Wonder Woman had been completely erased from its history. Issue 12 of the maxiseries sees

Wonder Woman blasted by the Anti-Monitor, which later in the same issue is explained as having devolved her, sending her backward in time to her original state as mere clay "spread . . . again across Paradise Island" (Wolfman and Pérez 354, 363). Pérez saw this treatment as indicative of how Wonder Woman was generally viewed at the company. As he points out, they let her, their most prominent female superhero, be eliminated from continuity with no plan on how to bring her back. Contrast this with Superman, originally slated to die as well in *Crisis* but granted a stay of execution precisely because, as Pérez notes, they had no plan to bring him back (Lawrence 76). Thus, the same circumstances preventing Superman's demise failed to prevent Wonder Woman suffering a more ignominious fate.

DC allowing Wonder Woman to be killed off in *Crisis* is not just indicative of how she was viewed at the time but also of a rather distaff position she occupied at DC for much of her existence. Despite the feminist intentions of her original creators— psychologist William Moulton Marston, his wife Elizabeth Holloway, and their paramour Olive Byrne—Wonder Woman's fortunes began to wane following Marston's death in 1947. As Cocca points out, "by the mid-1950s, . . . Wonder Woman, was a shadow of her former self. Softer and more feminized in appearance, she and female side characters such as 'Superman's girlfriend' Lois Lane portrayed women as far more oriented toward marriage, like the popular romance books of the time, than toward fighting injustice" (8). Robinson similarly notes how the post-Marston era not only emphasized romance over mission in late 1940s and 1950s *Wonder Woman* but also, in doing so, was "uncritically echoing social norms and attitudes it never occurred to them to challenge" (76). Nor would Wonder Woman's fortunes fare any better in later years. Like with much of the comics industry in the 1950s, and in response to a shrinking market as well as the infamous attacks by Fredric Wertham that led to Congressional hearings as well as a self-imposed Comics Code Authority, *Wonder Woman* plots veered into fantasy geared toward children but removed from contemporary and thus potentially controversial issues (Austin and Hamilton 50–51). Stories in subsequent decades often bordered on the nonsensical, a further testament to the little care DC put toward its most prominent female hero.

Nowhere is this lack more evident than in the convolutions surrounding Steve Trevor in the 1970s and 1980s. Trevor was murdered by the henchmen of Dr. Cyber in *Wonder Woman* no. 180, part of a feminist reboot attempted by writer Dennis O'Neil and artist Mike Sekowsky. He was brought back first as an amnesiac product of Wonder Woman's imagination and then, via the magic of Aphrodite, as a repository for the merged soul of the god Eros, who was then brainwashed into thinking he was Trevor. Masquerading as secret agent Steve Howard, Trevor/Eros was murdered yet again in *Wonder Woman* no. 248. But in *Wonder Woman* no. 270, a Steve Trevor from another reality crossed into the DC universe, and thanks again to another Hippolyte-induced amnesia, Wonder Woman and he shared adventures until 1984 when Hippolyte's and Aphrodite's manipulations were revealed. Eros was then pulled from the original Steve Trevor's body and replaced by the memories of the alternate Trevor with whom Wonder Woman had been most recently paired (Lapine-Bertone). To put it mildly, Wonder Woman's continuity was a mess, but the fact that it was allowed to be such a mess is the more troubling fact. On the one hand, *Crisis* gave Wonder Woman—and, for the most part, Pérez—a clean slate, but on the other hand, her erasure and thus need to be rehabilitated as a character was just the latest in a long line of ways DC had paid great disservice to her character.

Pérez taking over *Wonder Woman* had a lot to do with this rehabilitation, beginning with the ways in which he swerved from the original plans for the reboot. Pérez was not the first writer attached to the series. Instead, Greg Potter, with whom Pérez would share co-plotter credit for the first two issues, was originally slated as writer with a completely different artist. But as Pérez tells it, there was little enthusiasm for the intended direction of the series, particularly from women working at DC:

There wasn't a single woman working at DC who was happy with the direction they were going to be going with Wonder Woman, including the editor. It was like, well, they had the writer; they didn't particularly care for what he [wanted] to do, but right now there was no one else. They had an artist on there who was probably more known for drawing cheesecake, so chances are you're going to be getting a lot of gratuitous T&A shots of a character who's supposed to be a feminist icon [at least] to some degree. (Baker 57)

When Pérez took over the title, he did not eschew all of Potter's plans. He credits Potter, for example, for the idea of "the Amazons being reincarnations of women murdered throughout prehistory" and for how "Ares would be the first major threat that prompted Diana to go to Man's World" and Boston specifically, which was Potter's hometown (Pérez et al., *Wonder Woman* 8). Other aspects of Potter's plan were abandoned, largely based on Pérez's sense of how they did a disservice to DC's most prominent female character. Potter also intended the Amazons, according to Pérez, to have been "reincarnated with a total anger and hostility towards men" (Baker 59). Pérez similarly rejected a part of the plot that would have had Wonder Woman suffer an attempted rape upon first arriving in "Man's World" and thus seeking aid in a priest-run shelter for wayward girls (58–59). Pérez also grounded the series in Greek mythology more significantly than Potter, an emphasis that Pérez continued throughout much of his run.

Particularly because of this grounding in Greek myth, Pérez's work on *Wonder Woman* again puts him in parallel with Kirby: Pérez exhibits a similar kind of mythopoetic vision as that which Hatfield credits Kirby with possessing. As Hatfield explains, Kirby treats "the superhero as a vehicle for high fantasy and science fiction. Mythopoesis—uninhibited world-building—was the order of the day" (107). With *Wonder Woman*, Pérez engages in world building not unlike Kirby. Pérez, particularly after Potter's departure, had a clean slate with which to recreate Wonder Woman and her mythos. It is important to note that, within the new, post-*Crisis* continuity, Wonder Woman debuted in the present day of the DC Universe, that is, in the 1980s. There was now no World War II/Golden Age–era Wonder Woman, nor was there a Silver Age version (in the rebooted continuity, Black Canary/Dinah Lance replaced Wonder Woman as the sole female founding member of the Justice League of America). Thus, Pérez's recreation of Wonder Woman and her mythos was quite "uninhibited," to use Hatfield's term. Alongside Pérez's parallel to Kirby in this kind of vision is another form. As Hatfield elaborates, "Kirby's grand-scale mythic take on the superhero helped revitalize the periodical comic book . . . by inspiring an ongoing act of creation: the continual building and rebuilding of a fictive universe shared by scores of creators and hundreds of thousands of devout readers" (10). Here, Kirby's vision inspires those creators that came after him to add on to the mythos he established, which the iterative nature of comics continually builds and rebuilds and even restarts over and over. Speaking to this version of Kirby's mythopoetic vision is how, as many would agree, Pérez established the definitive version of Wonder Woman. It is Pérez's version that subsequent creators at DC can be seen as building on and revising within and in response to the larger fictive universe that is the DC Universe. Much of the film version of Wonder Woman portrayed by Gal Gadot in the DCEU derives from what Pérez established in his run. If, conceptually, Wonder Woman still owes a great debt to her original creators Marston, Holloway, and Byrne, modern/contemporary versions owe almost as great a debt to Pérez and his vision of DC's most prominent female hero.

One clear way in which it is possible to demonstrate Pérez's accomplishment, particularly in relation to gender, is via a comparison of his revised origin story with that penned by Marston, Holloway, and Byrne. One of two changes that are immediately apparent is the Amazons' appearance. To say that the Amazons in the Golden Age tale do not dress as warriors would be an understatement. The first two, introduced on pages 1 and 2 of the issue (including, as we find out on the next page, Diana), are dressed in dark-red bikini tops and lime-green pleated skirts that end about mid-thigh. The chief doctor wears a skimpy top—white, collared around her neck with cutouts for her shoulders and around the sides of her lower torso—and a knee-length white skirt. When readers are introduced to Queen Hippolyte, she too wears a bikini top with conical shapes protruding from each breast (not unlike those worn by Madonna at one point) and a long, flowing red skirt that extends to at least her calf (Marston et al. 8–9). Pérez's Amazons are quite differently attired. A panel of Hippolyte on page 15 of Pérez's first issue, where she prepares to confront Heracles, makes this clear. She is armored practically from head to toe: she wears a golden helmet with a mohawk plume in its center, a golden breastplate, bracelet, and leg sheaths in addition to a leather skirt. Only her upper arms and upper legs are completely uncovered (Pérez et al., *Wonder Woman* 27). This armored look is by and large common among the Amazons; when dressed otherwise, they favor long flowing gowns or short toga-style dresses that tend less toward cheesecake than what their Golden Age counterparts sported.

The second immediately apparent change is the role Steve Trevor plays in the origin. Pérez significantly reduces Trevor's importance. The Golden Age origin actually starts with Trevor's plane crashing on Paradise Island and the injured Trevor being discovered by Diana and her Amazon companion (Martson et al. 8). In Pérez's version, Trevor does not even appear until the series' second issue; by that point, Diana has already competed in and won the contest that will lead to her leaving Paradise Island and, eventually, becoming Wonder Woman. In the original, Diana's infatuation with Trevor motivates her to compete in the contest to determine who will accompany Trevor back to America. She falls in love with him practically upon sight and remains enamored with him during his stay on Paradise Island despite his being unconscious the entire time. In the reboot, Diana's motivation is dual: to combat the Greek god of war, Ares, as well as find a purpose as an Amazon. In a three-panel sequence at the bottom of page 27, she complains to herself about her sheltered life, feeling treated more as a child than a fellow Amazon, and prays to the gods for more, for purpose (Pérez et al., *Wonder Woman* 39). This is a far cry from the lovesick Diana who originally traveled to Man's World to remain with Trevor. Further underlining Trevor's much more incidental status in the new origin is issue 2: Diana, within the first three pages of the issue, brings the still-unconscious Trevor with her to the United States. There, he is abruptly (and off panel) dropped off at the Air Force hospital while Diana begins her quest (70–71).

It is, though, on Pérez's depiction of Diana/Wonder Woman herself that his run's representation of gender most crucially hinges. Pérez describes his effort in the series as one intended to "investigate the female psyche" in addition to elevate Wonder Woman as a feminist icon and thus to a similar status alongside Superman and Batman as part of what would eventually be referred to as DC's "Trinity" (Nolen-Weathington 53). Though the ability of Pérez to truly investigate women's psychological nature in the series may be questionable, scholars generally praise the series for its feminism. Cocca, for example, lists the various changes Pérez made as a reflection of third-wave feminism's continued emphasis on achieving equality for and ending discrimination against women (38). Robinson says much the same about various modern versions of Wonder Woman, among which Pérez's would be included (8). García credits Pérez with reinvigorating the feminist intentions of Wonder Woman's original creators while, as pointed out above, eliminating some of the more problematic aspects of her origins (164). These feminist intentions were foremost in Pérez's mind as he came on to the title. In his interview with Heidi MacDonald, done at a point when Pérez was thinking of his run on *Wonder Woman* as just one six-issue storyline, he made quite clear what he wanted to accomplish: "to show the reason why Wonder Woman is not the female Superman, as most people who are not familiar with this character think. By having her go through a gauntlet, showing not only her strength and her agility and everything else, but the things that make her an Amazon—love, wisdom, understanding" (29). One can see the ways in which Pérez came on to the title wanting to celebrate femininity. For one, he sees value in Wonder Woman that is unique to her rather than based on her simply being a female version of one of DC's most prominent male heroes. Similarly, whereas her original creators emphasized love as the essential female/feminine trait, Pérez provides that as well as wisdom and understanding as features unique to Diana and also as part of the femininity he wished to explore and elevate.

Much of what Pérez accomplishes with Wonder Woman derives from his visual presentation of her, which attempts to offer a depiction less based in overt sexualization. This intention is clear from the very cover of Pérez's first issue, where what seems emphasized is her strength. She stands, her legs wide apart and firmly planted, torso straight, head arched back, and arms crossed at the wrist above her head. The first issue closes with a similar image as Diana presents herself to the Amazons after winning the contest (figure 3.3). Here, she stands on a pedestal, left leg straight and behind a slightly bent right leg, torso straight, her head now looking down with a smile on her face, and arms again crossed above her head (Pérez et al., *Wonder Woman* 11, 44). Of course, her costume remains much the same and thus potentially problematic. Pérez's art does what it can to overcome this. For one, it is consistently depicted as akin to a one-piece bathing suit, with the classic star-spangled briefs below her belt and the red chest piece with an emblem both eagle- and W-shaped.

To better highlight how Pérez eschews more overtly sexualized depictions of her costume, one has only to look at *Wonder Woman Annual* no. 1, a jam issue that Pérez wrote but that featured multiple artistic contributors. One of the more strikingly different depictions is by Art Adams, who illustrated the six-page story "The Diving Bird." An image of Diana and her fellow Amazons on the first page depicts them in much more sexualized terms (figure 3.4). What with Pérez are Diana's classic star-spangled briefs become much more thong-like, as they are cut high on both her left and right, exposing not just her thighs but her hips as well. Various

Figure 3.3. Diana's first appearance in the Wonder Woman costume from *Wonder Woman*, vol. 2, no. 1, 1987 (Pérez et al., *Wonder Woman* 44).

Figure 3.4. Wonder Woman and the Amazons by Art Adams from *Wonder Woman Annual*, vol. 2, no. 1, 1988 (Pérez et al., *Wonder Woman* 534).

Amazons are similarly dressed; instead of wearing the short skirt that Pérez more commonly draws them with, two in particular have their toga-style outfits ending like Diana's in a high-cut thong with just a little ruffle at the top. Though the tops all the gathered Amazons—including Diana—wear are a much less formfitting, toga-style blouse, this does little to counteract Adams's much more sexualized depictions: the women's long and bare legs are much more prominent than anything else in the panel (Pérez et al., *Wonder Woman* 534).

Such sexualized depictions of female superheroes in general and Wonder Woman in particular became more of the norm following the end of Pérez's run on the series. Most infamous is the stint by writer William Mesner-Loeb and artist Mike Deodata Jr., which was very much part of the "bad girl" craze of the 1990s. Cocca characterizes the art of this "bad-girl" era as featuring skimpy, revealing costumes and "anatomically impossible proportions or anatomically impossible poses" or, at times, both (11). Cocca contrasts such art with the so-called "good-girl" art of the 1940s and 1950s, "in which attractive women were sometimes objectified" and depicted as "voluptuous" without the revealing outfits, sketchy anatomy, and provocative posing of later years (11). Pérez's *Wonder Woman* falls, chronologically, in between the "good girls" of the 1940s to '50s and the "bad girls" of the 1990s, and his visual depiction of women in the series likewise falls in between but is much more akin to the "good" than the "bad." Though there is no getting around the revealing nature of Wonder Woman's base costume, Pérez's art stops well short of making this costume even more sexualized than it is. Similarly, Pérez's Diana is much more realistically proportioned than with other artists. Again, Adams provides a useful contrast. In his depiction, Diana's legs are easily twice as long as her torso, whereas Pérez's Diana has legs only slightly longer than her upper body, as demonstrated in any number of panels and pages. And though there is a great deal of nudity in Pérez's run, it is always tastefully done, suggestive rather than explicit. On pages 9 and 10 of Pérez's first issue, the Amazons, when reborn, emerge from the water fully naked but are depicted from behind or the side where arms and/or hair or conveniently placed plants obscure their breasts and genitalia (Pérez et al., *Wonder Woman* 21–22). Once Diana settles herself in Man's World, there are several scenes of her praying to various gods and goddesses, during which she is nude. One such example comes from page 10 of *Wonder Woman* no. 15, where she prays to Eros to help her with her confusion over her attraction to Superman. In the first panel, we see her naked form, but it is entirely shadowed but for the glint from her bracelets. In the next three panels, she is only drawn from her head down to just above her breasts: in the first, from behind; in the second, from her waist up and with her hair covering most of her figure; and finally, from just her shoulders up in the third. The sequence ends with her being discovered by young Vanessa Kapatelis. In the remaining panels on this page, Diana's naked body is completely blocked by Vanessa in the second, and the pair are again depicted fully shadowed in the third (355).

Pérez similarly avoids the kind of overtly sexualized posing that was predominant in the "bad girl" era: "unnaturally twisted and arched to display all of their curves in front and back simultaneously" and, regarding Wonder Woman specifically, "falling out of the top of her costume and arching her thonged backside up in the air" (Cocca 12). As Cocca goes on to explain, "Female superhero bodies in action show strength and sexiness at some times, but in such poses their power is undercut as the reader is prodded to see them primarily as sex objects" (12). Pérez, when drawing Wonder Woman in action, largely avoids such sexualized posing and, in fact, more often draws his heroine in ways that emphasize her strength and power at least as much if not more than her sexiness. The cover and splash pages from *Wonder Woman* no. 1 discussed above are two clear examples of this. The cover to issue 4, which has her in battle against the creature Decay, is another image in which she is posed to emphasize her power and strength rather than sexual appeal: she is positioned in profile, swinging her right arm at Decay while the monster grasps her left; she leans forward into the punch, her torso turned slightly toward the reader but hips and legs firmly to the side and thus in no way unrealistically showing both her breasts and butt (a.k.a. the "brokeback" pose). In the actual battle with Decay within the issue, Pérez again poses her heroically rather than provocatively. As she captures a toppling statue before hurling it at her opponent or as she launches herself toward Decay, Wonder Woman, under Pérez's pen, always appears strong and determined rather than as a piece of eye candy for the reader (Pérez et al., *Wonder Woman* 91, 100, 102). At one point, Pérez even goes so far as to turn the "cheesecake" tradition on its head: on page 7 of issue 14, as Diana carries Heracles out from under Paradise Island, she cradles his, but for a tiny loincloth, naked form, legs pulled up toward his chest, a pose perhaps more "beefcake" than "cheesecake" but still atypical in superhero comics (329). Appearing similarly scantily clad throughout the series is

Pérez's version of the Greek god Hermes. Wearing only a yellow skirt and red cape that hangs off his shoulders and across his upper chest, Hermes, like Heracles, is consistently depicted in a greater state of undress and thus more sexualized than the female characters (with the exception perhaps of Cheetah, who appears fully nude but for her feline form).

Not to say that every image Pérez crafts is perfect in this regard. In issue 19, "The Witch on the Island," Diana is captured by Circe, chained, and tortured. One particularly provocative panel comes on page 6 of the issue, where Circe blasts Diana with some kind of mystic energy. Though Diana's figure is completely in shadow, her back is arched to such a degree that her breasts jut prominently, and the curve of her buttocks is emphasized (Pérez et al., *Wonder Woman* 443). But images like this are rare exceptions to the majority of Pérez's run, which much more often presented Wonder Woman as a figure of strength and power than as an object to be ogled.

As the above example shows, Pérez's art does not fully escape the pull of problematic attitudes or assumptions regarding gender afloat in the 1980s. Nor does his writing. Two subplots stand out as especially retrograde. The first involves Wonder Woman's mother, Hippolyte. In Pérez's first issue, on pages 17–18, Hippolyte is duped by Heracles, imprisoned, and raped while her fellow Amazons are likewise raped and/or slaughtered by Heracles's army (Pérez et al., *Wonder Woman* 29–30). Heracles then returned in the Challenge of the Gods storyline that ran from issues 10 to 14 of the series (and was, in fact, the storyline with which Pérez originally pitched his run on the title). And with Heracles's return came a disquieting storyline centered on Hippolyte forgiving and even falling in love with her rapist. Issue 12 saw Hippolyte following Wonder Woman/Diana past the Doorway of Doom to beneath Paradise Island, where various monsters and demons dwell; at the end of the issue, she finds Heracles turned to stone but still able to feel pain, such as when Hippolyte, not yet realizing it is him, lodges her battle-axe within Heracles's stone body (297). The next issue picks up from Hippolyte's realization, as she declares, on the very first page, to the trapped Heracles, "For centuries I hated you—but my years on Paradise Island have taught me the folly of such anger" (299). And though she initially turns her back on Heracles's plight, not much later and upon reuniting with her daughter, Hippolyte decides she must rescue Heracles. The dialogue on page 9 underlines her need to forgive her attacker: "I cannot allow anyone to suffer like that—not even he who so horribly wronged me those long centuries past" (307). This culminates in a sequence where Hippolyte is similarly tormented by Heracles's suffering, and via the magic of Diana's golden lasso, the two become linked so that each can receive "new knowledge, new insights" as well as feel and ultimately release each other's suffering, shown agonizingly on page 16 of the issue (314). Throughout these issues, the constant emphasis is on Hippolyte's compassion for and resulting need to forgive Heracles, her rapist.

The same theme then plays into the denouement of this storyline, which played out over the first nine pages of issue 14. Wonder Woman, returning to beneath Paradise Island from the events of the crossover in *Millennium*, finds a now-freed Heracles bracing himself against the weight of Paradise Island, protecting the unconscious form of Hippolyte. After bringing her mother back to her fellow Amazons, Diana also saves Heracles, whisking him from the depths beneath Paradise Island and back to the surface. Once there, Heracles addresses the assembled Amazons, listing his various crimes against them (though, notably, not explicitly apologizing for them) before asking them all for forgiveness, which they promptly acclaim (Pérez et al., *Wonder Woman* 323–31). Thus Heracles, with a minimum of contrition, is forgiven by all the Amazons on Themyscira. Though this is unsettling enough, a final exchange between Heracles and Hippolyte on page 15 of the same issue goes further. Alone with her in the woods, Heracles asks for a "kiss of forgiveness" (337). Hippolyte replies, "Aye, you have earned that, Heracles—and more!" Pérez goes on to underline her desire for Heracles with "I am still a woman, after all—and it has been a very long time!" (337). Quite literally, Hippolyte has gone from hating the rapacious Heracles to desiring him physically, a desire the dialogue emphasizes as inherently female. The next issue, which deals in large part with Diana/Wonder Woman's developing attraction to Superman, reiterates the love developing between Hippolyte and Heracles as Diana wonders, on page 10, "if my feelings for Superman are the same as those my mother harbors for Heracles!" (355).

Unsettling as this romance plot between Hippolyte and Heracles is, its trivialization of rape is not unique during the 1980s. In particular, it cropped up a few times on daytime soap operas. Probably the best-known example was *General Hospital*'s Luke and Laura. Their wedding in 1981 was a pop-culture phenomenon, but the romance leading up to that event was preceded by a drunken Luke's rape of Laura. Another popular 1980s soap opera, *Days of Our Lives*, used a similar device. Character Jack Deveraux rapes his wife, Kayla Brady, when he learns of her affair. Though Kayla does not subsequently fall in love with Jack, the series did eventually work to redeem Jack when he proved popular with viewers, eventually pairing him romantically with another character, Jennifer Horton, herself a victim of rape. Additionally, there's the nefarious scene in the first *Revenge of the Nerds* (1984) movie, during which the character of Lewis dons the Darth Vader costume of the cheerleader Betty's boyfriend in order to have sex with her. When he reveals his identity, though, Betty is nonplussed by the sexual assault. Similarly, in John Hughes's *Sixteen Candles* (1984), the passed-out character Caroline wakes up after having been carried off by Anthony Michael Hall's character with no memory of what happened the night before except a feeling that she "liked it." Though perhaps not quite as heinous as these examples, Pérez's Hippolyte/Heracles storyline still plays on a similar trivialization of rape.

Less egregious but still tapping into gendered discourses of the 1980s is a subplot involving supporting character Etta Candy. To his credit, Pérez much improved on Candy's original Golden

Age incarnation. There, Etta appears as a short and plump young woman (often accompanied by her fellow sorority sisters, the "Holiday Girls") as much known for her love of chocolate as for her spirited nature. In the early 1980s, Candy was reinvented as an Air Force Lieutenant but still trapped in any number of gendered stereotypes: insecure about her weight and playing roles of secretary and cook. Pérez's version hews relatively closely to this latter version. She's again an Air Force Lieutenant, serving as attaché to Steve Trevor in this case. She still, however, trades in a number of gendered roles. For example, as Trevor monologues on the first page of *Wonder Woman* no. 2, he complains about Candy's concern for him, describing her "more like my mother than my attaché" (Pérez et al., *Wonder Woman* 46).

But by far the greatest emphasis on Etta Candy, even in this reboot, is regarding her weight. In issue 5, as Diana thinks to herself on page 9 about how different those she's encountered in "Man's World" are from those in her experience growing up in Themyscira, she uncharitably comments on Etta: "She is a woman, even as I am— / and yet she is so stout, so unfit—! She seems wide enough to be two of me!" (Pérez et al., *Wonder Woman* 123). Later issues picked up on this thread, as Etta begins a weight-loss regime that hearkens to the diet-crazed 1980s. As Joan Ormrod explains about the era, both "diet and exercise industries emerged. Selling the perfect body was a consumer project and facilitated by exercise books and home videos" (127). In issue 14, the scene shifts from the aftermath of Diana's rescue of Heracles to, on page 11, Trevor and Candy at his childhood home. She climbs into the attic to let Steve know dinner is almost prepared, adding that Steven's aunt "even made a special diet plate for me" (Pérez et al., *Wonder Woman* 333). The diet subplot continues in the next issue, as Pérez presents a scene on the top half of page 17 of Etta undergoing a physical exam. She's congratulated on the thirty-five pounds she has lost, though she remarks about having twenty more pounds to go; furthermore, the examining medic, though stating that she's "within acceptable parameters now," also says losing that additional weight "couldn't hurt," closing with "You're turning into a real Wonder Woman!" (362). That this entire diet storyline coincides with the start of a romance plot between Candy and Trevor—their first kiss coming in the same attic scene—only adds to its problematic nature. Particularly troubling are Etta's thoughts following the medic's comparison of her to Wonder Woman, wondering how she is supposed to compete with the Amazon princess (and this despite the ways in which Pérez attempts to preemptively rule Trevor out as a love interest for Diana). Another mention of this subplot occurs in issue 17 as Wonder Woman travels to Greece. On page 7, as Trevor and Candy watch from the terminal, the former asks the latter what her plans are for the rest of the day, and she replies that she had planned on going to the gym, what with fifteen more pounds left to lose (398). This repeated charting of Candy's weight loss—her goal of fifty-five pounds, loss of thirty-five with twenty and then fifteen left to go—not only ties into 1980s diet fads but likewise stirs up gendered insecurities about women's bodies that remain largely untroubled while Pérez wrote and drew the *Wonder Woman* series even as the majority of his efforts subverted similar gendered norms both within comics and society.

Beyond *Wonder Woman*:
Gender in the Late Stages of Pérez's Career

Just as concerns regarding gender and its representation ran through Pérez's stints on both *The New Teen Titans* and *Wonder Woman*, these same concerns remain a throughline for the remainder of his career. That career hit a bit of a bump once Pérez left *Wonder Woman*, with several projects—the original *JLA/Avengers* intercompany crossover, a Titans graphic novel, and *The Infinity Gauntlet* series for Marvel—failing to come to fruition or Pérez having to bow out of the artistic duties prematurely. Even projects he completed—such as the Hulk series *Future Imperfect* and *Sachs & Violence* for Marvel's Epic line (both collaborations with

Peter David)—were a struggle for the artist to complete. Pérez experienced frustration over his struggles, both in terms of meeting deadlines and achieving the quality of art he wanted during this time (Lawrence 94). Even so, whether explicit or implicit, an attention to gender and women's representation (with not entirely unmixed results) continues through these difficulties and beyond.

Perhaps most indicative of the difficulties Pérez faced during this period, as well as the ambivalences within his depiction of women, is his effort to launch his creator-owned series *Crimson Plague*. Originally conceived as Plague, a villain to a character called Gladiator (which originated from an earlier Batman idea), the character was reworked into a protagonist, and the setting shifted from the present to the future. The first issue was released by Event Comics in 1997; however, Pérez's finances did not allow him to follow that release up with a second issue, and the series was shelved for three years. Then, Pérez helped form Gorilla Comics and attempted to resurrect the series there. However, finances again interrupted the series as backing for Gorilla Comics fell through and the creators involved found themselves shouldering production and promotion costs, a fact that allowed Pérez to only reprint an expanded first issue and the series' second issue before folding *Crimson Plague* up again (Lawrence 117, 119).

Besides these financial roadblocks, the series is, at best, mixed in its representation of women. On the positive side, a feature of the title was Pérez's basing the characters on people in real life, such as the title character, who was modeled after a woman Pérez met named Dina Simmons, and the main adversary in the title, whose appearance took after a dancer in a school Pérez's wife attended. In this, Pérez can again be seen as further pushing himself to individuate his characters. As he explains: "It was a great challenge to me as an artist to draw a book where . . . I have to go to a reference file in order to draw those faces accurately. I learned a lot about drawing faces on *Crimson Plague*" (Nolen-Weathington 71, 73). At the same time, the concept behind the Crimson Plague character proved problematic. Her "body served as a living vessel for one of the deadliest toxins known to science. A single drop of her blood—the plague from which she took her appellation—could kill a man almost instantly" (Lawrence 117). When Simmons asked Pérez about how this might affect things when the character menstruates, the series' depiction veered into what Singer describes as "tasteless" ("George Pérez" 304).

Far more successful—both financially and in terms of representation—was Pérez's return to the title that in many ways launched his career: *Avengers*. Paired with writer Kurt Busiek, Pérez helped restore the luster to *Avengers* as the series was rebooted following the demise of the Heroes Reborn line that replaced the original volume of the series. Robinson spends a significant amount of time, in *Wonder Women: Feminism and Superheroes*, discussing the Busiek/Pérez era of *Avengers* in terms of its being both postmodern and postfeminist. However, with the exception of describing Pérez's redesign of the Scarlet Witch's costume—"long red gloves, a red bustier that pushes her breasts upward into a deep cleavage and leaves her midriff bare, and low-slung harem pants with chains at the hips"—Robinson confines her commentary largely to plot developments and thus privileges the verbal aspect of the comic's narrative (120, see also 118–25). More inclusive of Pérez are Carolyn Cocca's thoughts on his and Busiek's depiction of Carol Danvers/Warbird (now known in comics and the MCU as Captain Marvel). Cocca specifically contrasts Pérez's depiction of Danvers with that by *Uncanny X-Men* artist Jim Lee. Lee's depiction is "emblematic of the early 1990s Image/Bad Girl style" as she is "scantily clad and posed in unnatural positions" (Cocca 194). Though still wearing her infamous "black bathing suit with a lightning bolt" that all too easily lends itself to overtly sexualized depictions, Danvers in Pérez's hands eschews this temptation. Cocca traces Pérez's Danvers back to his Wonder Woman, both women being drawn with their "curves fully covered and facing front heroically," making Danvers again "look entirely different" from Lee's version (196).

Other aspects of Pérez's stint on *Avengers* connect it to his ongoing concern with women's representation in superhero comics.

Both Cocca and García highlight Pérez's efforts on *Wonder Woman* to emphasize her Greek heritage and multicultural identity over the American nationalism that long underpinned the character (Cocca 37; García 164); he makes similar efforts regarding the Romani heritage of the Scarlet Witch. Besides the costume Robinson describes above, Pérez dresses Wanda in civilian attire similarly intended to evoke her heritage: midriff-baring tops or peasant blouses, flowing skirts, headscarves with various beaded chains, and bracelets as accessories. He likewise draws her with curlier hair and more defined facial features, such as a sharper chin and jaw line in place of her previously largely rounded characteristics. As well, throughout his almost three years on the series, Pérez continued his effort to differentiate female body types and faces that he began while on *The New Teen Titans*. Three female Avengers—Carol Danvers/Warbird, Wanda Maximoff/Scarlet Witch, and Angelica Jones/Firestar—were rostered during the first half of the Busiek/ Pérez series. In the first team shot at the end of issue 4, Pérez clearly differentiates the three women. Though Warbird and Scarlet Witch appear to have a similar build and height, Wanda's sharper features are clearly set against Danvers's wider and rounder visage. Pérez likewise distinguishes these two adult women from the younger Firestar, as the latter has a narrower frame, shorter and more slender legs, and an even rounder face. As Cocca states regarding Danvers/Warbird, all three women, though possessing the exaggerated curves of most female superheroes, are largely not sexualized, mostly covered, and consistently posed heroically. A change in roster a little over two years into the series sees Firestar depart the team, but the Wasp and She-Hulk rejoin. As before, the final team shot on page 21 of the issue (no. 27) showcases even more dramatic differences in these women's appearance. Though Warbird and Scarlet Witch again appear even in height, here the former has longer legs and a shorter torso, while the latter is longer in torso and shorter in legs. Wasp, though at the front of the team, appears slightly shorter than these two women and with a slightly slimmer body. She-Hulk, of course, towers above the other three and with a much broader and muscular form (Busiek and Pérez 2: 21).

The 2012 *Worlds' Finest* title launched as part of DC's New 52 reboot featured not only DC's Power Girl and Huntress but Pérez as a contributing artist.[8] With a plot split between the characters' present-day adventures on the newly rebooted Earth and flashbacks to their arrival from their original Earth-2, *Worlds' Finest* has Pérez paired with artist Kevin Maguire, the latter handling the flashbacks, while Pérez penciled the present-day escapades. The contrast between the two further highlight the ways in which Pérez eschews overly sexualized depictions of women superheroes. Maguire's art—treading the line between "good girl" and "cheesecake" comic art—depicts both women with the soft and rounded aesthetic that is his hallmark. The statuesque Power Girl/Karen Starr, too, is often depicted, both in her superhero and civilian lives, in short skirts and tight-fighting tops and dresses that emphasize her ample breasts. On Pérez's pages, though there is perhaps not as much variation in height and body type between the two women as we might expect, they are less sexualized. This is likely due, in part, to them appearing most often in their full-body costumes when Pérez draws them, but he somehow manages, on page 8 of the series' first issue, to make Power Girl seem less of a cheesecake figure than Maguire despite the fact that her costume is almost entirely in tatters (Levitz et al. 8).

It is Pérez's final work, the six-issue *George Pérez's Sirens* series published with Boom! Studios, that finds him as a creator putting gender and women's representation at the fore in a way that hearkens back to his *Wonder Woman* run.[9] Pérez, in fact, draws a direct line between that earlier work and this series: "*Wonder Woman* was my watershed in that regard [i.e., serving a female audience]. . . . It inspired me that when [I] finally got to do a creator-owned book it would be a very female-centric [one]. I love to explore the female experience" (qtd. in Wilkins). Further connecting the series to *Wonder Woman* as well as his subsequent work, Pérez continues his pattern of basing his female characters on real people. As he explains in another interview, "Every Siren, and much of the supporting cast, is modeled after a real person, many of them cosplayers" (Diestch). The models Pérez utilizes include not only, as he says, several cosplayers but also his wife and niece. The series is a dizzying mash-up of science fiction, time travel, fantasy, and other genres built around the titular team of female superhumans working with a team of largely female scientists (and, of course, alien space dragons) to restore the human race and the Sirens' names as they are believed to have caused the destruction of Terra Prime (a.k.a. Earth) a century before the series takes place.

What by now should be perceived as hallmarks of Pérez's depiction of female characters are again on display in *George Pérez's Sirens*. Foremost among these is his diversification of female body types from the comic book norm. To that end, the first two characters depicted are the Siren mystic Fanisha, modeled after Pérez's wife and sporting gray hair and slightly broader features than her teammates, and head scientist Prof. Falgout, who is reminiscent of Pérez's Etta Candy in being more heavyset and older though younger than Fanisha. There is not as much body diversity among the rest of the Sirens, however; a panel on page 13 of the series' second issue depicts four Sirens—Agony, Ammo, Kage, and Skywire—as they don their respective costumes. It shows them all to be of similar shape and frame. Only Agony, a warrior/berserker, appears slightly taller and broader than the rest, and all evidence the roundness of form that was more prevalent in Pérez's early work. To balance this similarity, though, Pérez does give each woman defining character traits. Ammo is perhaps the most nuanced, having previously been the team's assassin now turned pacifist and struggling throughout the series with what being a Siren requires her to once again do. The team's putative leader, Highness, likewise struggles with her desire to possess the blade she stole from Sirens' enemy Perdition, her inability to let it go jeopardizing the team's efforts to restore themselves and Earth. Highness, too, recalls plot elements of Pérez's *Wonder Woman*, as the reader first encounters her having been enslaved and sold to men to be physically and sexually tortured; the first image of her, on page 9 of the series' first issue, silhouetted but clearly nude and held up by chains, cannot help but recall Hippolyte's capture and enslavement by Heracles, though that plot's dubious forgiveness plot is pretty quickly dispatched as, on page 13 of the same issue, Highness uses her chains to turn the tables on her would-be rapist (Pérez et al., *George Pérez's Sirens*).

The time travel element of the series similarly allows Pérez to comment on, however briefly, issues not only of gender but also of violence and racism. Ammo, having been displaced in time into 1880s Arizona and as a schoolteacher named Miss Bishop, underlines a critique of Indigenous displacement. When, on page 7 of issue 1, one of her students repeats his father's justification for displacing Indigenous tribes due to the violence they presented, Ammo/Bishop exposes that rationale as a mere disguise for other exploitative motivations. Gender and race similarly come together in 1949 Alabama where the computer interface Sherita is sent, taking on the form of an African American maid unable to speak or write and suspected of carrying on an affair with her male employer, Nathan Jessee. When Highness arrives to transfer Sherita's cybernetic consciousness to the present, readers learn that, far from having an affair, Sherita was aiding Jessee in the technological advancement that is the basis for his family's apparent wealth. As the radio signal that Sherita surreptitiously created in 1949 to contact Highness explains, Jessee "preferred to be suspected of marital infidelity rather than reveal that his technology skills were advanced with the aid of a Negro domestic" (originally issue 1, page 17; see Pérez et al., *George Pérez's Sirens*). The series' second issue uses another Siren's jump to the past—this time the Japanese swordswoman Kage to 1754 Japan—to make a similar point about gendered assumptions. When a male samurai arrives at her house of courtesans demanding to be taught "the art of shadow combat," he dismisses the women and Kage in particular as mere geishas, unable to believe that a woman can be the master he wishes to learn from (issue 2, pages 8–9; see Pérez et al., *George*

Pérez's Sirens). While not achieving the critical and popular heights of his work on *Wonder Woman* and other series, *George Pérez's Sirens* does demonstrate the creator's continued desire to appeal to a female audience generally underserved in comics. It likewise at least attempts to address and counter issues of gendered and other forms of violence and exploitation by moving female super-humans and their adventures to the center of his work, a pattern of effort that maintains for the majority of Pérez's career in comics.

Conclusion

George Pérez's Sirens series was George Pérez's final work. He announced, on Facebook in 2019, his retirement from comics due to a series of health issues, diabetes and cataracts having plagued him for years (Grunenwald). Then, less than two years later, Pérez announced his diagnosis of stage-three pancreatic cancer, foregoing treatment in order to enjoy his remaining time with family, friends, and fans (Couch). A little over six months after revealing his diagnosis, Pérez passed away at home on May 6, 2022, at the age of sixty-seven (Burke).

After both his diagnosis and death, tributes from comics fans and professionals began to populate social media. The sheer number of these tributes, as well as their passion and veneration, testifies further to the significance and effect of Pérez's career and work on fans of all stripes. Industry tributes were similarly fast in coming upon Pérez's death. In April's *Avengers* no. 55 (2022), Marvel repurposed an earlier-published Pérez page featuring various Avengers raising their glasses in toast; the top of the page reads "George Pérez" and "Once an Avenger . . . always an Avenger." In June 2022, DC ran a two-page tribute titled "DC Celebrates George Pérez" in all their titles. The image features Pérez seated and surrounded by the DC characters he was most associated with, drawn in his style by twenty-six different artists. Pérez, the New Teen Titans, and Deathstroke were fittingly drawn by José Luis García-López, who followed Pérez as artist on the second volume of *The New Teen Titans* and is, like him, one of the most prominent Latinx artists of the 1980s. (Prior to this, the two rival publishers had collaborated on publishing a limited edition reprint of the long out-of-print collection of *JLA/Avengers*, managing to even get a copy to Pérez prior to his death). The final two issues of DC's *Teen Titans Academy* (2021–22) offered a further tribute, as the Titan Chupacabra met his "Uncle Jorge," a bearded, tropical-shirt-wearing artist. Two moments in issue 15 stand out. In the first, Uncle Jorge tells his nephew that he's leaving for the West Coast and retirement despite their having just met. He says, in words that likewise reflect on the untimeliness of Pérez's death: "I know the timing sucks, but I'm trying not to get bogged down by it. Let's just be grateful for the moment we've had—and make the most of what's left!" (Sheridan and Derenick 11). And near the issue's end, Chupacabra gazes at the portrait of himself in his uncle's sketchbook, whispering, "Thanks, Maestro," a term of endearment often applied to Pérez (17).

Pérez left behind over forty years of comic art and storytelling, leaving, as this book has argued, an indelible but underrecognized stamp on the form. Pérez's wish, as he expressed in many interviews, was "to die with an unfinished comic book page on my drawing board" (Baker 87). Though Pérez's wish did not come true, what does remain "unfinished" is fully exploring and explaining George Pérez's legacy within comics: from the style and possibilities inherent within the comic book page to how, through what those pages depict, Pérez contributed to understandings of marginalized persons and bodies and likely more. Pérez left fans, creators, and scholars a significant legacy that has only begun to be reckoned with in terms of what he, as a creator, accomplished.

NOTES

1. Marston's wife, Elizabeth Holloway-Marston, as well as Olive Byrne, the niece of feminist and birth-control advocate Margaret Sanger who lived with the Marstons in a polygamous relationship, were both inspirations for Wonder Woman and aided in the character's development. For more on their relationship and its connections to the early feminist movement, see Lepore.

2. Pérez, in his use of these triangular and trapezoidal panels, demonstrates some influence from Neal Adams, who similarly broke with the traditional grid of the comic page. Pérez in fact talks about how, when showing his early portfolio of comic art at conventions, Adams was foremost among those who "pretty much excoriated" his work (Nolen-Weathington 14).

3. Singer, for example, details how the density in Pérez's and other "Bronze Age" comic book artists' style was a product of increasing narrative complexity, shrinking page counts, and balancing these both at a time of increasing costs ("George Pérez" 293).

4. There are those, however, who downplay the significance of narrative story-worlds. Lisa Zunshine, in *Why We Read Fiction*, casts descriptions of storyworld spaces as something at best tolerated or at worst skipped over in narrative (26); Alan Palmer goes further, discounting the existence of an objective storyworld within a narrative, seeing it more as the subjective product of individual character narratives within the larger one (141). Both Zunshine and Palmer privilege representations of consciousness over other representations in narrative, which, as I explain elsewhere, likely contributes to their downplaying of storyworld spaces in narrative (Hamilton 112–13).

5. All citations for the Busiek and Pérez *Avengers* series come from the two-volume omnibus collection. As neither volume identifies page numbers, those pages referenced in the text and/or citations—here and throughout the remaining chapters—are for the individual issues being discussed.

6. In truth, and as revealed much later in the series, Garrett was given the powers of Cold War Marvel hero the 3-D Man, which had been stolen by the Triune Understanding's leader, Jonathan Tremont.

7. As a result of launching the second volume of *The New Teen Titans*, the first volume was retitled *Tales of the Teen Titans* but continued the numbering from the original series. *Tales* presented new stories featuring the Titans through issue 58, at

which point it began reprinting the second volume until issue 91, when it was then canceled.

8. As Levitz et al., *The Lost Daughters of Earth-2*, volume 1 of *Worlds' Finest*, does not identify page numbers, all page references in the text and/or citations are for the individual issues being discussed.

9. As Pérez et al., *George Pérez's Sirens* does not identify page numbers, all page references in the text and/or citations are for the individual issues being discussed.

WORKS CITED

Alaniz, José. *Death, Disability, and the Superhero: The Silver Age and Beyond.* UP of Mississippi, 2014.

Alaniz, José, and Scott T. Smith. "Introduction: Uncanny Bodies." Smith and Alaniz, pp. 1–34.

Aldama, Frederick. *Latinx Superheroes in Mainstream Comics.* U of Arizona P, 2017.

Aldama, Frederick. *Your Brain on Latino Comics: From Gus Arriola to Los Bros Hernandez.* U of Texas P, 2009.

Austin, Allan W., and Patrick L. Hamilton. *All New, All Different? A History of Race and the American Superhero.* U of Texas P, 2019.

Baker, Bill. *George Pérez on His Work and Career: A Conversation with Bill Baker.* Rosen, 2008.

Bukatman, Scott. *Matters of Gravity: Special Effects and Supermen in the 20th Century.* Duke UP, 2003.

Burke, Minyvonne. "Legendary Comics Book Artist George Pérez Dies after Cancer Battle." *NBC News*, 7 May 2021, https://www.nbcnews.com/pop-culture/pop-culture-news/legendary-comic-book-artist-george-perez-dies-cancer-battle-rcna27792.

Burroughs, Todd Stevens. "The Spy King: How Christopher Priest's Version of the Black Panther Shook Up Earth's Mightiest Heroes." Darowski, pp. 103–19.

Busiek, Kurt, and George Pérez. *Avengers.* Omnibus vol. 1, Marvel, 2015.

Busiek, Kurt, and George Pérez. *Avengers.* Omnibus vol. 2, Marvel, 2015.

Claremont, Chris, et al. *The Deadly Hands of Kung Fu.* Omnibus vol. 2, Marvel, 2017.

Cocca, Carolyn. *Superwomen: Gender, Power, and Representation.* Bloomsbury, 2016.

Couch, Aaron. "George Pérez, Legendary Comic Book Artist, Diagnosed with Pancreatic Cancer." *The Hollywood Reporter*, 7 Dec. 2021, https://www.hollywoodreporter.com/movies/movie-neeorgerge-perez-artist-cancer-1235058463/.

Darowski, Joseph J., editor. *The Ages of the Avengers: Essays on the Earth's Mightiest Heroes in Changing Times.* McFarland, 2014.

David, Peter, et al. *Incredible Hulk Epic Collection: Future Imperfect.* Marvel, 2017.

Diestch, T. J. "Despite Eye Surgery, George Perez Keeps His Focus on 'Sirens.'" *CBR*, 3 June 2014, https://www.cbr.com/despite-eye-surgery-george-perez-keeps-his-focus-on-sirens/.

Doležel, Lubomír. *Heterocosmica: Fiction and Possible Worlds.* Johns Hopkins UP, 1998.

Englehart, Steve, et al. *Avengers Epic Collection: Kang War*. Marvel, 2022.

García, Enrique. "The Latina Superheroine: Protecting the Reader from the Comic Book Industry's Racial, Gender, Ethnic, and Nationalist Biases." *Comic Studies Here and Now*, edited by Frederick Luis Aldama, Routledge, 2018, pp. 163–79.

Gray, Jonathan W. "'Why Couldn't You Let Me Die?' Cyborg, Social Death, and Narratives of Black Disability." *Disability in Comic Books and Graphic Narratives*, edited by Chriss Foss, Jonathan W. Gray, and Zach Whalen, Palgrave Macmillan, 2016, pp. 125–39.

Grunenwald, Jen. "George Pérez Announces His Retirement from Comics." *The Beat*, 19 Jan. 2019, https://www.comicsbeat.com/george-perez-retirement/.

"Hall of Fame." *Comic-Con*, https://www.comic-con.org/awards/hall-fame-awards ?page=9. Accessed 26 Sept. 2023.

Hamilton, Patrick L. *Of Space and Mind: Cognitive Mappings of Contemporary Chicano/a Fiction*. U of Texas P, 2011.

Hanson, Marit. "Mistress of Cyberspace: Oracle, Disability, and the Cyborg." Smith and Alaniz, pp. 95–110.

Harvey, Robert C. *The Art of the Comic Book: An Aesthetic History*. UP of Mississippi, 1996.

Harvey, R. [Robert] C. "In Search of Perez's Storytelling." Heintjes, pp. 58–63.

Hatfield, Charles. *Hand of Fire: The Comics Art of Jack Kirby*. UP of Mississippi, 2012.

Heintjes, Tom, editor. *Focus on George Pérez*. Fantagraphics, 1985.

Herman, Brian. *Story Logic: Problems and Possibilities of Narrative*. U of Nebraska P, 2002.

hooks, bell. *Black Looks: Race and Representation*. South End Press, 1992.

Lapine-Bertone, Joshua. "The Many Strange Deaths and Rebirths of Steve Trevor." *DC*, 18 Jan. 2021, https://www.dc.com/blog/2021/01/18/the-many-strange-deaths -and-rebirths-of-steve-trevor#.

Lawrence, Christopher. *George Pérez: Storyteller*. Dynamic Forces, 2006.

Lepore, Jill. *The Secret History of Wonder Woman*. Alfred A. Knopf, 2014.

Levitz, Paul, et al. *The Lost Daughters of Earth-2. Worlds' Finest*, vol. 1, DC Comics, 2013.

MacDonald, Heidi. "The George Perez Interview." Heintjes, pp. 8–39.

Marston, William Moulton, et al. *Wonder Woman: A Celebration of 75 Years*. DC Comics, 2016.

Moench, Doug, et al. *The Deadly Hands of Kung Fu*. Omnibus vol. 1, Marvel, 2016.

Morrison, Grant. "Morrison Manifesto." *New X-Men*, by Morrison, Ultimate Collection, vol. 3, Marvel, 2008, pp. 1–10.

Nolen-Weathington, Eric. *George Pérez. Modern Masters*, vol. 2, TwoMorrows Press, 2007.

O'Connor, Lauren. "More than a Retcon Replacement: Disability, Blackness, and Sexuality in the Origin of the Operator." Smith and Alaniz, pp. 111–24.

Ormrod, Joan. *Wonder Woman: The Female Body and Popular Culture*. Bloomsbury, 2020.

Palmer, Alan. *Fictional Minds*. U of Nebraska P, 2004.

Pérez, George, and Cliff Biggers. *The Art of George Pérez*. IDW, 2012.

Pérez, George, et al. *George Pérez's Sirens*. Boom! Studios, 2018.

Pérez, George, et al. *Wonder Woman*. Omnibus vol. 1, DC Comics, 2015.

Revenge of the Nerds. Directed by Jeff Kanew, performances by Robert Carradine, Anthony Edwards, Timothy Busfield, Curtis Armstrong, Larry B. Scott, Brian Tochi, Julia Montgomery, and Ted McGinley, 20th Century Fox / Interscope Productions, 1984.

Robinson, Lillian S. *Wonder Women: Feminisms and Superheroes*. Routledge, 2004.

Ronen, Ruth. *Possible Worlds in Literary Theory*. Cambridge UP, 1994.

Sacks, Jason. "Earth's Mightiest (Dysfunctional) Family: The Evolution of *The Avengers* Under Jim Shooter." Darowski, pp. 31–44.

Sheridan, Tim, and Tom Derenick. *Teen Titans Academy*. Vol. 1, no. 14, DC Comics, June 2022.

Sheridan, Tim, and Tom Derenick. *Teen Titans Academy*. Vol. 1, no. 15, DC Comics, July 2022.

Shooter, Jim, et al. *Avengers Epic Collection: The Final Threat*. Marvel, 2013.

Shooter, Jim, et al. *Avengers: The Korvac Saga*. Marvel, 2010.

Singer, Marc. "'Black Skins' and White Masks: Comic Books and the Secret of Race." *African American Review*, vol. 36, no. 1, spring 2002, pp. 107–10.

Singer, Marc. "George Pérez and the Classical Narrative Style." *Inks*, vol. 4, no. 3, 2020, pp. 288–308.

Sixteen Candles. Directed by John Hughes, performances by Molly Ringwald, Anthony Michael Hall, and Justin Henry, Universal Pictures / Channel Productions, 1984.

Smith, Scott T., and José Alaniz, editors. *Uncanny Bodies: Superhero Comics and Disability*. Pennsylvania State UP, 2019.

Wilkins, Jason. "A Love Letter to Fans: George Perez Discusses His New BOOM! Studios Series 'Sirens' and the Creative Process." *Broken Frontier*, 17 Sept. 2014, https://www.brokenfrontier.com/love-letter-fans-george-perez-discusses-new-boom-studios-series-sirens-creative-process/.

Wolfman, Marv, and George Pérez. *Crisis on Infinite Earths*. Deluxe Edition, DC Comics, 2–15.

Wolfman, Marv, et al. *The New Teen Titans*. Omnibus vol. 1, DC Comics, 2017.

Wolfman, Marv, et al. *The New Teen Titans*. Omnibus vol. 2, DC Comics, 2018.

Wolfman, Marv, et al. *The New Teen Titans*. Omnibus vol. 3, DC Comics, 2018.

Wonder Woman. Directed by Patty Jenkins, performances by Gal Gadot, Chris Pine, and Robin Wright, Warner Bros. Pictures / DC Films / Atlas Entertainment / Cruel and Unusual Films, 2017.

X-Men. Directed by Bryan Singer, performances by Patrick Stewart, Ian McKellan, Hugh Jackman, Famke Janssen, James Marsden, Halle Berry, and Anna Paquin, Twentieth Century Fox, 2000.

Yurkovich, David. "The Secret Origin of Bill Mantlo." *The Deadly Hands of Kung Fu*, by Chris Claremont et al., omnibus vol. 2, Marvel, 2017, pp. 12–13.

Zunshine, Lisa. *Why We Read Fiction: Theory of Mind and the Novel*. Ohio State UP, 2006.

INDEX

ABOUT THE AUTHOR

Patrick L. Hamilton is professor of English at Misericordia University in Dallas, Pennsylvania. His previous books include *Of Space and Mind: Cognitive Mappings of Contemporary Chicano/a Fiction* and, with Allan W. Austin, *All New, All Different? A History of Race and the American Superhero*. He has contributed chapters to edited collections on comics, including *The Routledge Companion to Gender and Sexuality in Comics*; *Graphic Borders: Latino Comic Book Past, Present, and Future*; and *Multicultural Comics: From Zap! to Blue Beetle*. With Allan Austin, he cohosts *Even More Mashed Up*, a podcast on contemporary popular culture.

Printed in the United States
by Baker & Taylor Publisher Services